Toward Dawn

Spiritual Opportunities in a World of Doubt

Peter Mills

John Hunt
Publishing Limited

Copyright © 2004 John Hunt Publishing Ltd
46A West Street, Alresford, Hants SO24 9AU, U.K.
Tel: +44 (0) 1962 736880 Fax: +44 (0) 1962 736881
E-mail: office@johnhunt-publishing.com
www.johnhunt-publishing.com
www.0-books.net

Text: © 2004 Peter F. Mills
Design: Nautilus Design

ISBN 1 84298 141 2

A CIP catalogue record for this book is available from the British Library.

Printed in Singapore by Tien Wah Press.

Contents

Preface

One of the prompts for this book derives from a particularly pointed verse in Edward Fitzgerald's translation of the *Rubaiyat of Omar Khayyam*.

ONE MOMENT IN ANNIHILATION'S WASTE
ONE MOMENT OF THE WELL OF LIFE TO TASTE
THE STARS ARE SETTING, AND THE CARAVAN
DRAWS TO THE DAWN OF NOTHING – OH MAKE HASTE.

Fitzgerald's elegantly crafted message stands in sharp contrast to the hope of eternal life that is offered by the Christian Churches. Wherein lies the truth? If we seek an answer, do we wonder at the dawn of nothing, or at the dawn of eternity?

This is only one among a number of issues explored, but it shares the fairly common fate of being afforded no single assured answer. The problem is doubt, elemental doubt attaching itself tenaciously to many parts of the argument. But is doubt, no matter how heavy or persistent, a good reason to abandon the quest for answers? A vigorous negative response underlies this book. Upon its basis a range of questions is examined: spiritual, religious, philosophic and scientific.

The actual existence of uncertainty raises a further question. What opportunities for spiritual life are available to those for whom the great issues of life, death and eternity are suffused with doubt? A substantial part of this text is taken up with the attempt to answer. One outcome is the recognition that spiritual paths in an uncertain world will be many rather than few. The task of finding an appropriate path must rest with each individual; the hope for these thoughts is that they may provide some pointers.

Although the argument is broadly sequential as it proceeds through its ten chapters, individual chapters can also be read separately, with only occasional cross-referencing. Chapter 1, which is mainly scientific and philosophic, precedes the consideration of spiritual issues. Chapter 2 is chiefly concerned with scene-setting, and Chapter 3 stands out somewhat as dealing with the nature and limitations of knowledge. Thereafter the focus is maintained upon spirituality and the sequential nature of the argument gradually becomes stronger.

Peter F. Mills

1
Reality

The Limits of Science

When Descartes embarked upon his project of pure enquiry, he took for his starting point the celebrated, 'I think, therefore I am.'[1] As the thoughts that follow are less austere than pure enquiry, they can start from a rather more expansive position. To begin with, I perceive as well as think, and I make decisions, which means that I possess free will. In fact, I engage in a number of other activities as well, but it is convenient to leave them for a later exploration. Perceiving, thinking and deciding are enough to make a start. There are also a great many other people in the world, and they too are in the business of perceiving, thinking and deciding (and doing other things as well). The world itself is physical and objective – it is still there even when none of us is looking at it. Non-realists do not believe this, but most of us do, and it is included in the start.

In modern times, our thinking about reality has been greatly influenced by developments in physical science. At the practical and technological level these developments have been of immense value, but conceptually they can lead our thoughts into serious blind alleys. This can happen particularly when the subject of concern is our mental relationship with the physical world. To grasp the problem, consider the following assertion:

Free will is incompatible with modern universal science.

This will not be readily accepted. Before attempting to justify it, some preliminary questions need to be answered concerning meaning. To explain terms, 'free will' in this context means the capacity to choose between two or more different courses of action. The expression 'modern universal science' embodies the notion that a single set of scientific laws accounts for the behaviour of everything in the physical universe.

To begin the argument, it is evident that we live in a scientific age. Science is compulsory for our children in school. Persons with scientific qualifications occupy important professional positions in industry, government and academia. What is more, whether scientifically trained or not, we participate in a remarkably common approach to the physical world that we observe around us. We accept, virtually without hesitation, that its behaviour is determined by the presence of scientific laws. Suppose, for example, that a stone is dislodged from the top of a cliff by the action of wind and rain. We feel entirely confident that the laws of gravitational attraction and aerodynamics, operating together, will determine just how the stone will fall to the beach below. Furthermore, if applied mathematicians can express those laws in the form of equations, then, given details of cliff, stone and wind, we accept that they will be able to calculate the exact point at which the stone will strike the ground. The stone may get there before the calculation, but that will not interfere with the principle or the belief! This approach to the physical world derived initially from the work of Sir Isaac Newton, from far back in the seventeenth century.[2] Nevertheless, in what has since become known as Newtonian Dynamics, it continues to be applied right up to the present day to all objects and systems in the common scale of observation.

Now it gets trickier. If, instead of a substantial object like a stone, we consider something altogether smaller, like an electron, then the laws of modern science cease to be exact and deal instead in probabilities. The laws relating to the stone are deterministic – determining just where the stone will land. On the other hand, the laws relating to the electron are only probabilistic – offering different probabilities for different positions where the electron may be found. These laws belong to Quantum Theory.[3] It seems strange, but that is how modern physics says that it is when things are sufficiently small, and mostly we are minded to accept modern physics.

What happens if we move up the scale from elementary particles like electrons toward visible objects like stones? How do probabilities and determinisms come together? Scientists are not entirely agreed on the matter, and it is not clear that they are going to resolve it at all quickly, but roughly speaking it seems to work like this. A stone includes many billions of electrons and other elementary particles. If all their probabilities are taken together, they 'smear out' into the seemingly exact deterministic result that obtains at our ordinary level of observation. Or something like that! Anyway, the important thing is that when we deal in sticks or stones or other 'ordinary' things, providing only that we know the situation at the beginning, then the laws of science enable us to say exactly what is going to happen. And at risk of labouring the point, because the laws are deterministic there is only one thing that can happen!

Now consider a variation of the story of the cliff. Suppose a small boy who is walking near (but not too near) the cliff-edge spots a tempting stone lying on the grass in front of him. He has a choice. He can pick up the stone and toss it over the cliff, or he can walk by and leave it alone. Now comes the crunch! Given a common starting point, it is not possible for both of his alternative courses of action to take place in accord with the deterministic laws of science. If one of them accords, then the other does not!

This is such a straightforward point to make, and yet in large measure it is simply ignored. Moreover, when it does get explored, the tendency in the scientific world is to dismiss it as quickly as possible.

The scientific community is uncomfortable because it puts awkward question marks against the proposition that scientific laws apply without interruption throughout the physical universe. But consider the previous example a little more closely. Suppose the boy, the stone and the cliff are regarded as a closed physical system. 'Closed' just means that nothing happens outside the system to interfere with the progress of events. His mother does not call him for lunch just as he is about to pick up the stone! So the boy makes his decision, picks up the stone and throws it over the cliff. If the laws of physical science are universal, then everything that happens (to boy, cliff and stone) does so in accordance with those laws. Fine. Now suppose that instead the boy decides to leave the stone where it is and walk on along the cliff. The same set of universal physical laws, operating from the identical starting point, cannot also account for this alternative course of action. Something, somewhere must be different!

There are two fairly well-explored negative responses to this assertion. The first consists of denying that the starting point is the same in both cases. The mental state of the boy differs slightly in one case from the other immediately before he decides what to do. This difference is expressed physically by slight (almost imperceptible) differences in his brain state. From the two different starting points, the two different courses of action flow, with everything duly explained by the appropriate laws of science. The snag of course is that this denial of a common starting point also does away with the notion of free will. The boy does not genuinely make a choice. He may appear to, but the reality is that, from two different initial states, he simply does what the physics and chemistry in his head obliges him to do. So that kind of solution, although it works perfectly well in its own terms, only does so at the expense of denying the very existence of individual decision-making – of the exercise of free will.

The second response is to appeal to Quantum Theory to explain how the two different courses of action could both fall within the compass of scientific law. The idea is that the two different decisions, viewed physically as two different brain states acquired from a common starting point, can both be accounted for as probabilities within the scope of quantum variation. This argument can seem quite beguiling, but upon closer examination it becomes evident that it does not work. To use a different example, suppose a person, James say, chooses to place a coin 'heads' up on a table. He could alternatively spin the coin, and by chance (one chance in two) it may settle showing 'heads'. Another person arriving after the event would not be able to tell whether the coin was 'heads' by choice or by chance. But that does not mean that the two are the same. No chance was involved in the deliberate placing of the coin by James. So choice and chance are fundamentally different, even though the distinction may not always be apparent. To return to the boy and the stone, once the stone is picked up by choice, then the question of probability, quantum fashion, can no longer apply.

So the making of decisions, the exercise of free will, cannot be subsumed within the physical realm and its scientific law. Does it matter? For the practical applications of science in engineering and technology, not a great deal! Computers work and aircraft fly uninfluenced by questions that link free will to the universality of science. (It would of course trouble people greatly if the same lack of universality extended into the actual machines, but that does not seem to be the case!) But where individuals are concerned, the issue is of far greater significance than is commonly appreciated. If scientific laws are the sole determinants of physical activity, then free will can only be an impression. We can no more choose a course of action than a person on a roller-coaster can decide where to go next. Our behaviour is determined by our physics and chemistry, so that decision-making, responsibility and moral judgement, are reduced to the status of myth.

Few people believe this, of course. Attitudinally we become split-minded. We think we are responsible moral beings able to take personal decisions in the course of our lives, and yet we simultaneously believe that deterministic or probabilistic physical laws explain everything that happens in the physical world. This is an unstable and unsatisfactory situation. Its paradoxical nature needs to be recognized and then challenged, however far that takes us from modern conventional wisdom.

This is an argument that has serious implications for philosophy and religion, as well as for modern science. In particular, it impacts strongly upon the ideas of creativity and the concept of human spirituality. These are all issues that will be taken up later. Before that, however, in finishing these opening remarks, let us return to the initial assertion that free will is incompatible with modern universal science in order to identify one immediate consequence. Assuming that free will is not to be abandoned, there are two possible ways forward for physical science. The first is simply to assert that physical laws do not apply universally throughout space. Some physical phenomena, arising when free will is exercised, have to be explained entirely without them. There are in this sense law-free zones in the physical world. The second less radical possibility is that, whilst physical laws (of a deterministic or probabilistic nature) continue to apply throughout the physical universe, they are just not sufficient in themselves to explain all the events that occur within it. Other influences deriving from decision-making are also present! Both of these inferences are consistent with the original assertion. Which one is correct remains to be discovered!

Body and Mind

The incompatibility of free will with universal science raises important questions concerning the relationship between body and mind. Once again it is appropriate to begin with Descartes, who famously declared that there was an ontological distinction between mind and body, a distinction that is usually described nowadays as Cartesian dualism. But while many people would follow Descartes by distinguishing in a commonsense sort of way between body and mind, at the higher reaches of science and philosophy there is a problem. Notwithstanding his abiding status as one of the world's greatest philosophers, Descartes' notion of the dualism of mind and matter has not prospered in recent times. Preference in modern argument attaches to physical monism, that is to say to the idea that the whole of reality has but a single ultimate physical nature. Furthermore, a good deal of popular, if confused, support attaches to this position. It is widely believed that the thrusts of modern science, particularly developments in information technology, artificial intelligence and neuroscience, are all supportive of this view. This preference for physical monism embraces approach as well as conclusion. Descartes proceeded from belief in his own existence as a thinking being, a mind, to the conviction that his body also existed and was of a quite different nature from his mind. In contrast, modern monist thinking starts from the physical world, with bodies and brains as elements within it, and then endeavours to explain mind as an holistic property of the body.

This popular tendency to accept the monist position more or less without question can be illustrated by a personal anecdote from higher education, where much of my working life was spent. On the relevant occasion, I was teaching a class of computer science undergraduates. We were trying to distinguish between the ways in which computers and human beings process information, and it quickly became apparent to me that the students, virtually without exception, regarded the physical universe as the solitary basis for existence, and took it for granted that life, awareness and personal existence, were all grounded in and dependent upon physical reality. There were fields, elementary particles, and a space-time continuum in which they existed. And that was all! Just one student said somewhat diffidently that there might be something called the soul – implying that if there were, then it might belong to some category other than the physical – but he did not pursue the point and nobody else wanted to take it up. Perhaps this overstates their position. Perhaps some of the students did have doubts or questions but chose to leave them unremarked, because the occasion of the lecture did not appear appropriate to raise them. But that is not how it seemed, and the discussion was quite intense.

So dualism of mind and body has become fairly widely discounted, with physical monism ruling in its place. It seems, however, that this adoption of monism is altogether too facile, and is seriously undermined by the inability to sustain both free will and universal science. It is also compromised in other ways, including the difficulty of explaining how consciousness, the awareness of perception and thought, can be accounted for in a wholly physical system. These problems can best be explained with the aid of an example.

Suppose John opens a door to let James through. Then both body and mind are involved, and physical and mental events occur throughout the activity. The activity can be described sequentially as follows:

(a) John observes James approaching. This is an act of conscious visual perception.

(b) John thinks about the situation, perhaps in doubt whether to open the door. If not, this act of cognition may only take an instant.

(c) John decides to open the door, and acts immediately upon his decision. The decision is a conscious act of free will. He could alternatively have decided to leave the door closed. As it is, he successfully opens the door in order to admit James.

In stage (a), the observing of the approaching person is a matter of conscious perception. Modern natural science will explain the process in terms of light waves reaching the eye, and of signals in the form of minute currents travelling along the pathways of the nervous system from the eye into the brain. Upon receipt of the incoming signals the electrical state of certain neurons (brain cells) will be induced to change and further minute currents will flow within the network of the brain. In the process, chemical as well as electrical reactions are involved, and the result is the creation of a myriad of tiny signals. The basic question relating to this web of activity is this: What is there, over and above the complex signal-processing that is taking place, that constitutes the awareness or conscious perception of which John is the recipient?

Attempts to answer this question are legion, but, under the constraints of monism, none is wholly satisfactory. There is a basic difficulty. To obtain an answer, awareness has to be treated as an holistic property of the physical organism that is the brain. But the brain is composed of physical parts whose own general properties arise from the basic physical properties of mass, charge, energy, momentum and so on. However many there are, there is a sense that they are all of the wrong kind for the task in hand. To explain why, consider as an analogy the problem of trying to construct a musical instrument out of the parts of a telescope. The properties of a telescope are ordinarily those of an optical nature. To form a musical instrument, other quite different properties of an acoustic nature would need to be discovered among the parts of the telescope and then put to use. If a musical instrument were actually constructed in that way, its behaviour could only be explained by reference to the acoustic properties, not by any harking back to its original optical nature. Upon a similar argument, how could awareness and other properties associated with being the conscious mind of a person emerge from the behaviour of parts possessing only objective unconscious physical properties? There is no adequate answer, just an ongoing argument!

Similar difficulties apply at stage (b) above, the cognition stage. Cognition is a conscious activity, and as such it is no easier than perception to explain in merely physical terms. The problems of monism only reach their peak, however, when the question of free will is considered. This is reached at stage (c), with the actual decision by John to open the door and the subsequent action he takes to perform the deed. According to the physical monist, the decision will take the form of further electrical and chemical activity in the network of the brain, which in turn will cause tiny currents to flow in the nervous system of the body. These in their turn will activate the muscles necessary to move the arms and open the door. The question that arises is how the conscious action of taking the decision is involved in the process. As before, the response of the monist is that the decision is constituted holistically in the activity of the brain. This time, however, in addition to awareness there is the larger problem of finding a place for free will in a situation described only in terms of physical activity. As previously discussed, the basic problem of free will, John's free will in a monist physical universe, is as follows. If the physical world is deterministic and John is part of that physical world, and nothing more than part of it, then his behaviour must also be deterministic. And if that is the case, then his behaviour cannot include decision-making at all, in the sense of choosing freely between two different courses of action. In opening the door, John does what he is obliged to do, not what he chooses to do. That is the fundamental contradiction. In the monist context, it also becomes very difficult to argue that John can be held responsible (or blameworthy) for his action. In fact, it becomes very difficult to make any sense at all of the concept of morality, of actions being either good or bad.

The principal issue, then, relates to volition. The point at which the nature and relationship of physical and mental reality become critical is the point at which free will is exercised. If the monist argument is correct, if the physical universe is either deterministic or probabilistic (dependent upon chance), then the capacity to make autonomous decisions simply does not exist. Whatever happens, whether inside or outside the brain, is a matter of physical determinism or probability – decisions do not enter into it.

At this point a remark should be added concerning Systems Theory and the possibility of obtaining free will through emergence.[4] To explain the idea, in some extended forms of Systems Theory an emergent property is posited as a property of a whole system that is not dependent on the properties and relations of the parts. Could free will be such a property? The first problem is that there are serious question marks put against the actual existence of emergence. Even allowing the possibility, however, there remains a further fundamental problem. Normally a system that is deterministic at the level of its elemental parts will maintain that same characteristic at any higher level. Similarly, a probabilistic system at a low level will normally remain probabilistic at any higher level, although the probabilities may 'smear out' or average out at a higher level to yield an outcome very close to determinism. Unless emergence were somehow to escape that kind of constraint, it could not logically provide a basis for volition. Given the extent of the difficulties, whilst the possibility of monism delivering free will via emergence cannot be formally dismissed, it will not be taken any further in this text.

To summarize, one outcome of this survey is that the awareness of a conscious person cannot be given an adequate explanation within the constraints of the monist position. Where free will and decision-making are concerned, however, the outcome is much more striking. The argument for emergence excepted, free will is not just lacking an explanation, it is simply not possible!

Being unwilling to abandon free will, it follows that the dualist position, however unfashionable it may be in philosophical circles today, needs to be reconsidered. What is intended next is to put forward a series of positive and constructive remarks relating to it, and to follow that with an account of some of the immediate consequences. Given the nature of the subject, the detailed argument is complex in places, but the conclusions are available in summary form at the end of the chapter.

There are two immediate points. Dualism is normally taken to mean that the physical and mental, the body and the mind, belong to fundamentally different forms of existence. It is therefore a dualism of entities. There also exists, however, the intermediate concept of property dualism, forming what is roughly speaking a halfway house between physical monism and entity dualism or dualism proper. Expressed in systems terminology, there is one set of entities, with two kinds of property – physical and mental. These entities are identified physically by the senses, but strictly they should be treated as combined physical and mental entities, due to the duality of their properties. To distinguish property dualism from emergence, it is assumed that both the physical and the mental properties extend right down the scale to elementary particles. For example, electrons would possess mental as well as physical properties! This form of dualism cannot be disproved, but it is difficult to be very enthusiastic about it, because the problems of locating two such fundamentally different sets of properties in a single set of entities are immense. Intuitively, it seems more straightforward and satisfactory to accept dualism in full, and that means accepting the dualism of entities.

The second immediate point concerns Descartes' own assessment of dualism. Speaking about himself, Descartes asserts that he is a thinking thing, a substance whose essence it is to think.[5] Within the broad thrust of his argument, that is a reasonable enough assertion for him to make, but the problem with the words 'thing' and 'substance' is that they have a very physical ring to them. That may be just a quirk of translation, but arguably it is more than that. The 'thinginess' of things is a 'thinginess' that belongs to the observable world around us, and encourages us to approach minds as if they were just another set of objects. From that stance, it follows quite naturally to attempt the reductionist move to limit reality to just one sort of thing. So whilst following the general thrust of Descartes' argument toward dualism, the intention is to identify more emphatically the fundamental differences between the two categories.

Upon the strength of these initial thoughts, let us adopt the presupposition that, excepting a capacity for interaction, bodies and minds are wholly unlike one another. It follows that if bodies are objects, then minds are subjects, and if bodies are things, then minds are beings other than things. Associated with this presupposition is the thought that only when the fundamental differences between body and mind have been established can progress be made to explain their interaction.

What then does a dual reality contain? There is the mind, which resides in a mental domain, and which will be explored more widely in Chapter 2. There is also the body, including the brain, which exists in the physical domain.

The interaction between the physical and the mental would seem to take place in the brain, which constitutes the gate between the two forms of existence. Strictly speaking, the brain should be described as the physical component of the gate, the corresponding mental component being not perceivable by the senses or sensors of the objective world. It would also be prudent to regard the brain as being the principal gate between the physical and the mental, thus allowing the possibility of a weaker interaction elsewhere in the body, or perhaps even outside the body. How then does the brain-gate work, or more modestly, how could it work?

Moving cautiously, it is helpful to identify the dimensions that would be needed for a combination of physical and mental existence. From ordinary observation, physical entities (objects) exist in three spatial dimensions, x, y, z and one singly directed dimension of time, t. In order to interact with the physical world, mental entities (subjects) must also exist in, or at least touch upon, these same four dimensions. Mental entities will, however, live in a mental domain requiring one or more additional dimensions. For simplicity (and ignorance), just one further dimension, s, will be assumed for this text.

Secondly, there is a need to establish the possible modes of interaction between the physical and the mental. Suppose that the laws governing mind-free actions in the physical world are deterministic at the ordinary or macro-level, so that the state of a closed macroscopic physical system at some particular time instant is uniquely determined by its state at the immediately preceding time instant. In that case, mental activity could only influence events by a rank intrusion upon or suspension of the physical laws. For example, Newton's first law of motion that is normally expressed in the form, 'A body remains in a state of rest or uniform motion unless it is acted upon by a force', might require the term 'force' to be replaced by the expression 'force or thought'. Alternatively, the physical law or laws might simply cease to operate in the presence of a mental act. Whilst the former position seems the more coherent, it has to be said that evidence is simply not available at present to make an informed judgement between them.

The human brain itself comprises million upon million of neurons or brain cells, connected in a vast and complicated network of synapses. When a neuron fires it delivers a minute current into its output synapse. Its firing pattern is determined by the signals (currents) that it receives from its set of input synapses. The brain, or appropriate parts of it, also receives input signals from the various sensory organs of the body, and delivers output signals to the muscles in order to stimulate them into action. The ordinary expectation is that this whole complex activity takes place strictly in accordance with the relevant laws of physical science. When the mind makes a decision, however, and the body acts in accordance with that decision, somewhere down the line the relevant physical laws are either intruded upon by the mental activity, or are temporarily set aside as a result of the mental activity. That is the nature of physical and mental interaction. It is not what modern science encourages us to believe, and yet it has to be the case. The argument that has previously been rehearsed is not to be set aside.

Any attempt to move beyond the bare statement of the fact or reality of interaction is bound to be speculative. Very briefly, neurons would seem to provide the most obvious site for interaction. What would be required is a mental intrusion upon physical circumstance so that neurons fire that would not otherwise fire. That would seem the most straightforward way for decisions of the mind to be impressed upon the body. It may not be quite like that, of course, but something of the sort must take place. At this point in the argument, what matters is not the exact manner in which physical laws are intruded upon or set aside, but the very fact that such things happen at all. Reality is seen to be more subtle and complex than we are often disposed to admit!

Laws, Lawlessness and Creativity

The adoption of entity dualism requires a fundamental rethink of scientific principles. Where mind and body interact in the activity of volition, which is almost certainly the case in the brain and may also apply elsewhere, neither the laws of classical determinism nor quantum probability can continue to hold. From time to time, when decisions are taken, neurons will fire that scientific law requires should not fire. The dualist explanation is that certain decisions, made in dimension s, occasion physical acts that involve the overriding or replacing of physical law. Upon present interpretations, therefore, such decisions must be described as physically lawless.

It may be, however, that a more positive approach can be found. Consider as an analogy a billiards table upon which the one red and two white balls are moving. The movement of the billiard balls around the table can be calculated according to the laws of two-dimensional dynamics. But suppose one of the balls drops into a pocket? At that point the two-dimensional laws are no longer sufficient to account for what has happened. To be fanciful, imagine a person whose perception and understanding is limited to two-dimensional movement. He can give a perfectly good account of the movement of the balls around the table, describing it in terms of obedience to scientific laws, but his scientific explanation finishes when the ball drops into the pocket. All that he can do is theoretically ring-fence the pocket and declare it to be a zone in which scientific law ceases to obtain. But from our standpoint of three-dimensional advantage, we can see that scientific law still obtains, once the expansion of the action into three dimensions is accepted. It is not that the two-dimensional laws are wrong. It is simply that they need to be incorporated into the greater three-dimensional system.

The question arises: does a corresponding circumstance obtain when a neuron fires at an unfortunate moment? Are the pockets of the billiards table the analogical equivalent of the neurons of the brain? Can the laws of physical science be incorporated within a larger framework of law that includes physical and mental interaction? It is too early to offer a definitive answer, but it seems reasonable to pursue the possibility. Very briefly, the approach could be as follows.

Given the points already established, it is unavoidable that the laws of science, as normally understood, are not universally applicable. Their departure or overruling coincides with the interaction of the physical and mental to allow for the implementation of decisions. It may be that it has to be left like that, with the neurological activity associated with the making of decisions ring-fenced, and the laws of science applicable everywhere else. Without denying any of the previous points, however, there does remain the possibility of finding additional laws, operating within the ring-fence, which could combine with the presently understood laws of science to provide a wholly lawful physical domain. In so writing, 'law' is being used in the scientific sense of a law imposing deterministic or probabilistic behaviour in its sphere of application. Such a law of interaction might require, for example, that every time a particular person makes the mental decision to type the letter 'q' on his word processor, a particular and unique set of neurons fires up in his head. A law of this kind would differ from a strictly physical law in being related to the dualism of the physical and mental entities. As such, its deterministic nature would be directly evident only to the subject (mind) to which it related, and only then with great difficulty. It would be a law observable to others only via the assertion of the relevant subject.

Having briefly and rather speculatively explored the regime of interaction, it remains to examine the mental realm itself, the domain in which minds reside and decisions are taken. A general discussion of the self will be offered in Chapter 2, but the particular issue of decision-making in the context of scientific law is considered ahead of that discussion. The outcome is not comfortable!

In approaching the issue, it is necessary first to identify an important characteristic of scientific law, namely its relationship with causality. Induction and causality are the two principles that normally underlie our approach to the physical world. Neither of them can be proved. Nevertheless, we commonly believe that forces cause objects to accelerate, and that voltages cause currents to flow. We believe that gravitational attraction accounts for planetary motion. What we call the laws of science are in many cases simply our attempts to codify particular aspects of beliefs that we obtained through the application of induction and causality. It is true that, at the rarefied level of Quantum Theory, some doubts emerge about the presence of causality (although induction continues to apply), but that constitutes an unresolved exception. In general, the scientific approach is one that seeks to explain the phenomena of physical existence by recourse to cause and effect. Now comes the crucial point! When we explore decision-making in the mental domain, the underpinning of causality is no longer available. In fact, a decision cannot be lawful, if the term 'lawful' is restricted to the scientific sense of the codifying of causality. There can be no scientific laws in the mental domain, the domain of the decision-making mind, corresponding to the laws that we have uncovered in the physical universe. If there were such laws, then decision-making would no longer be free, which means that it would cease to be decision-making in the full and proper sense of the expression.

Decisions then are taken autonomously through the exercise of free will. Cause and effect does not have a role. For some scientists and philosophers, this is a source of great difficulty. The way forward in this argument is twofold. First, it is insisted that, because there is a fundamental ontological distinction between the mental and the physical, parallel considerations are rendered inappropriate. In particular, cause and effect, as understood in the physical world, cannot be directly applied to affairs in the mental realm. Secondly, and probably of even greater significance, within the mental domain the activity of decision-making is irreducible. Mental beings make decisions, and that is the explanation of how decision-making occurs. (In this connection, there could be a problem of terminology. Persons make decisions! It could therefore be claimed that a person is the cause of a decision, and thus the cause of any effects that stem from the decision. To use 'cause' in that way would of course be a major extension from previous usage in this argument. It is a possibility that is explored further in Chapter 2.)

Two further points need immediate ventilation. First the absence of laws of cause and effect does not entail the absence of laws of any kind, and, secondly, the freedom to take decisions does not deny the role of influence. For an example of both, in making a particular decision, a person may be profoundly influenced by a moral law. The law does not operate in the deterministic or probabilistic manner of a scientific law, it is not representative of cause and effect, but it is present in the mental domain and influences the decision that is reached. In reality, decisions are often subject to a number of different influences, but it is important to recognize that a genuine decision is not merely the weighted sum of the influences. A computer can perform in that way, and is sometimes casually regarded as making decisions, but such a process is not to be equated with the activity of a human mind in exercising free will.

Reverting to the physical world, the application of free will or volition involves the overriding of either the determinism of classical science or the probabilities of Quantum Theory. Whichever is the case, one thing remains the same – the world is not as it would otherwise have been. The natural order is disturbed. In essence this process is creative (or destructive). Whether it is a cook placing a pan in the oven, an artist bringing a brush to the canvas, or a gardener starting the motor mower, the operation of free will, the exercise of decision-making, must bring about creative changes in the world.

How does this compare with the situation in dimension s, the dimension of the mind? What is now asserted is that creativity is not compatible with law. As with the opening assertion in this chapter, this cannot be proved in any formal sense, but powerful arguments can be adduced in its favour. It should be added that the term 'law' in this assertion spans only those laws that are deterministic or probabilistic. The fundamental thought is that free will, not bound by law, is essential for creativity, invention, imagination, and almost certainly for intuition and induction. A computer can be programmed to draw pictures, but no one will regard it as being an artist. The reason is that creativity and artistry cannot be bound or controlled by rule, law or program. What is more, the converse is also true. Decision-making must have the capacity to be creative, responsible and moral, or else it is not genuine decision-making at all, but merely reduces to a form of algorithmic law-driven process, offering what is only a spurious impression of autonomy.

Creative (or destructive) decisions cannot be determined or even given probability ratings by previous circumstance. That being the case, what kinds of creativity can emerge? Clearly there is the creativity that finds expression in the physical world, the creativity that invents word processors, paints pictures or bakes bread. Such instances are frequent and important. But human creativity has the capacity to extend beyond physical activity to the actual development of the self. Arguments are persistent over the rival claims of nature and nurture in the determining of human character. No doubt both are influential, and the arguments about them will continue as endeavours are made to establish just how influential. But human beings can also be creative of themselves, or at least developmental of themselves, by the decisions they take. This applies particularly to decisions with a moral content, decisions that are taken under the influence of a moral law. Within this sense of internal development, sequences of moral decisions are likely to be the more important but there will be no decisions that are void of significance. It is fundamental to human nature to be autonomous, free and morally responsible. Human beings are therefore capable of being creative, not only in the objective physical world but also upon their own selves through the process of internal mental feedback from their decisions.

All this is much too fast and much too far for many scientists and philosophers. The essence of the claim is that a decision is unable to be lawful, at least in the deterministic or probabilistic sense. If it is, then it ceases to be a decision! It reduces to an event in a predetermined sequence, or an event in a sequence of probabilities. An essential characteristic of a decision is its freedom. It is the exercise of choice, not chance or programmed response. The principal objection to this position is lodged in the claim that, without causation to link a person, pre-decision, to the same person, post-decision, there can be no continuity of existence or permanence of character. The philosopher William James, to name a distinguished protagonist, regarded free will as a preposterous doctrine, within which a series of decisions reduced a person to a series of disconnected instants![6]

The point is serious and not easily overcome, but it does not disable the argument. In mathematics, a function does not cease to be a function merely because it is discontinuous. In like manner, a mind, a self, a mental being, does not cease to exist because of the discontinuities of decision-making. The mind certainly changes as a result of decisions, but that is not a disaster. What is there that does 'stand still' in this world? Almost every entity is subject to change with the passage of time, if only by deterioration, and is not expected to remain precisely the same in order to continue to be identified as the entity. Given the argument about self-development, it is not simply the person, pre-decision, who is responsible for a moral decision, but also the person, post-decision, the person of self-development, the person whose changed state arises specifically as a consequence of that same moral decision.

Reality in Outline

So a dualist account of mind and body, or at least of mind and brain, is able to yield a rational account of decision-making. It thus contrasts with a physical monism that can only proceed from decision-making into difficulties and outright contradictions. Accepting the dualist position, it becomes possible to identify the nature of reality, at least in outline terms. Before offering the outline, however, there is one remaining issue to be explored. What are the circumstances of animals and plants in a dualist existence? Are animals and plants physical entities only, or do they (or some of them) also share in the mental domain? There must be the likelihood that they do, but probably in ways that are more limited than those of humankind. Clearly there is scope here for a major study in its own right. It is beyond the reach of this text, however, so to make progress the fairly cautious assumption will be adopted that at least some animals may have a limited capacity for decision-making. The possibility that they (and plant life) may be participant in the mental realm in other ways will be left unexplored. With that limited thought included, it is now possible to list the elements of the dual reality that has been established. The list is as follows:

1. I exist as a self, a person, a mind, an autonomous individual human being in a mental domain, able to perceive, think, and exercise free will in the making of decisions.
2. An external objective physical universe exists, described informally as the world. It includes my brain and body. My mind interacts with the physical universe through my brain and body, but is distinct from it, so that reality is dual.
3. Other selves, persons, minds exist, akin to myself, and (at least some of them) are related to the physical universe in a manner similar to myself.
4. Excepting interaction with the mind, the behaviour of the physical universe is regular and coherent, satisfying the principles of induction and causation. The principles are given expression in scientific laws that are deterministic or probabilistic.
5. Minds interact directly with the external objective physical universe, chiefly and perhaps entirely, through the brain. This interaction impinges upon the otherwise deterministic or probabilistic behaviour of the world. The manner in which this occurs needs further exploration and elucidation. Where decision-making is concerned, however, the interaction is creative (or destructive) in the sense that events and states in the world are no longer as they would have been. In the mental domain itself, decision-making is not lawful, in the sense of laws that are deterministic or probabilistic.
6. The physical universe includes other living organisms (plants

and animals) besides those of human beings. The dual nature of reality impinges upon them, but in more limited ways than those of human beings. The subject needs further exploration.

The six articles leave many questions open, but do nevertheless provide a sufficient grounding in the nature of existence to enable these thoughts to be carried to the next stage. There is more to the self than perception, cognition and decision-making. In the next chapter, the endeavour will be made to look more widely at the question of just what it is to be human.

Notes

1. Translation of the original '*Cogito ergo sum*'. René Descartes, *Meditations*, 1641.

2. Sir Isaac Newton and Newtonian Dynamics. In his publication, *Philosophiae Naturalis Principia Mathematica*, 1687, Isaac Newton established laws of motion and gravitation, and expressed in mathematical form the dynamic behaviour of what at that time were the known aspects of the physical world. Described as Newtonian Dynamics, this approach to the analysis of the physical world held sway for the next two hundred years, until developments in Relativity and Quantum Theory put some of Newton's assumptions and conclusions in doubt. Underlying Newtonian Dynamics is the belief that, if the mass of an object and the forces acting on it are known exactly, then the subsequent motion of the object can be predicted exactly and explained exactly. This is determinism, and following Newton it became widely adopted in branches of science other than dynamics.

3. Quantum Theory. At the sub-atomic level uncertainties and probabilities prevail. According to the uncertainty principle of Werner Heisenberg, the more accurately the position of an elementary particle such as an electron is known, the less accurately can its velocity be measured. It follows that the continuing motion of an electron can never be predicted exactly. Instead, the position at which it will be observed at any future time can only be calculated in terms of probabilities. These probabilities are expressed mathematically by what is known as the wave function. What is radical about Quantum Theory is the proposition that, between observations, in some sense the electron *is* the wave function. A commonsense view would be that the electron particle must be at some particular but unknown point at any given moment between two observations, and that the wave function merely gives the probabilities. The radical view is that the electron is actually constituted by the wave function between observations, and only reduces to a particle at the making of an observation. The distinction is subtle, but the radical interpretation appears to be necessary in order to explain the outcome of various scientific experiments. The argument continues concerning the question of just what this viewpoint implies for the elemental nature of physical reality. For a book that explores these implications, see Euan Squires, *The Mystery of the Quantum World*, Institute of Physics Publishing, 1986.

4. Systems Theory. A system (physical or otherwise) is composed of parts. The parts have individual properties and also have relations, one with another. A

system as a whole has properties, and is externally related to its environment. Any part of a system is potentially a system in itself, and any system is potentially a part in a super-system, that is to say a system extending into the environment. An holistic property is a property that arises at the level of the whole system and does not appear at any lower level. A part/whole reductive system is one in which the holistic properties of the system can be explained in terms of the properties and relations of its parts. The theory of part/whole reductionism is that this process can be continued 'downwards' to the most basic parts (atoms in the philosophic sense) of which the system is composed. In a physical system, parts at the lowest level are formed by the elementary particles of which all physical things are composed. It follows that normally the holistic properties, the properties of the system as a whole, are ultimately dependent upon the laws of physics, the natural laws (of Quantum Theory) that apply to the elementary particles. In practice, the linkage from the behaviour of the whole system to the natural laws may be extremely difficult to obtain, and often quite unnecessary. In a more contentious part of systems theory, emergence is the idea that whole systems may have exceptional properties that cannot be causally explained by the behaviour of their parts. It follows that an emergent physical system, unlike a 'normal' system, could possess properties that are neither causally dependent upon the laws pertaining to particle physics nor explicable in terms of them. At this time, claims to demonstrate the existence of emergent properties are the subject of continuing argument. The possibility of emergence is not included in the conclusions of the main text.

5. Descartes, *Meditations*, 1641. The relevant text is to be found in the English translation by Haldane & Ross, Cambridge, 1911, vol. 1, p. 190.

6. William James, *Pragmatism*, 1907.

2

Human Being
Spiritual Being

Onward From Plato

We do not know when human beings first began to wonder about themselves, but we do have on record what was probably the first truly analytic description. The author was Plato, who famously described the self as being composed of three parts.[1] The parts comprised the appetite, spanning the range of human physical desire; the reason, embracing intellectual capacity and the creative talents; and finally what Plato termed '*thymos*'. In modern terms, it is less easy to identify just what Plato meant by *thymos*, but it certainly included the conscience, together with the heroic aspects of human nature. In 1992, at nearly the other end of philosophic history, Francis Fukuyama, in his study of 'the last man', makes much of *thymos*.[2] Encompassed within it, he finds the human desire for esteem, which he categorizes as being conceptually distinct from the desires of the appetite. Within *thymos*, Fukuyama distinguishes between the desire to be recognized as equal to others, and the desire to be recognized as superior to others. Fukuyama argues persuasively that it is the latter that can give rise to some of the very worst instances of human behaviour. In its various aspects, *thymos* is of quite fundamental importance to human nature. There will be much to say about it in later chapters.

Modern psychology also offers a division of the person into three parts, but this time the parts are those of reason, emotion and will. Additionally, the Church, at least up to fairly recent times, was wont to identify yet another division into three, talking about body, mind and soul – or body, mind and spirit. The division of body and mind has already been explored in Chapter 1, issuing forth in the adoption of the dual nature of existence. Questions relating to soul or spirit will be looked at later. The immediate focus will be upon the identity of the person or conscious self. A division into rather more than three will be required.

One consequence of considering a person divided into parts is that it does lead rather easily to a systems-type approach. What is argued here, however, is that a human being exists as a whole self and is not divisible in the systems way. Any talk that is systems-type should therefore be regarded as only 'so-to-speak'. As remarked in Chapter 1, a person is essentially a subject, not an object, and is thus a unified being in a way that defies objective part/whole analysis. The problem is that much of our ordinary language is framed around the idea of objects, and does not easily transfer into subjective mode. As ordinary language is what is available, however, the language of parts and systems will quite often need to be used, but with the overriding provision that it is only 'so-to-speak', as a person is essentially a unity, a subjective unity, and not a system of parts!

Perhaps a better way of applying part-type language is to think of it as describing a set of aspects or capabilities. Neither word is ideal, but 'aspect' will be used fairly often, with the connotation of the term extended to include 'capability'. (Not very scrupulous, but a warning has been given.) Each aspect of a person is distinct, but aspects are not parts. For example, a person may be unusually skilful at crosswords, wholly honest in making his tax returns, and extremely fond of Belgian chocolate. His crossword capability may be ascribed to his reason, his honesty in respect of taxation to his conscience, and his liking of chocolate to his appetite! But all this merely constitutes a convenient way of addressing three different aspects of the same person, not a means of describing three different parts of the same system. That at any rate is the basis upon which this argument will proceed.

Beginning with Plato, nearly always a good idea, a human being, a self or person, comprises a reason, an appetite, and a *thymos*. In fact, a self is a good deal more complex than that, but Plato's threefold self makes a useful start. *Thymos* presents an immediate problem. Conscience is a notion that we are at home with in modern terminology, but *thymos* is more than just conscience. To overcome the difficulty, both conscience and 'heart' will be placed within the span of *thymos*, with the term 'heart' cunningly defined so as to cover all those aspects of *thymos* that do not fit into the ordinary sense of conscience. So moral issues are a matter for conscience, but questions of love, compassion and caring, to give important examples, are all matters for the 'heart'.

What then of the human will, the capacity for autonomous decision-making? In Plato's three-part person, the presence of the will is implicit, and must be taken to belong in some unifying way to all three parts. This idea is helpful in so far as it supports the rejection of a systems approach to selfhood, but in other respects is less satisfactory, as it fails to attach sufficient importance to the actual nature of free will. In the modern threefold account of man, the will is separately identified. This is one point where modern thinking and the present argument concur happily. As reckoned here, the will is so fundamental to the actual being and activity of a self that it does need separate identification, albeit with customary cautionary comments about a division of the self into parts being only 'so-to-speak'. To be precise, the reason, appetite, conscience and 'heart' can all be regarded as exercising their influence upon the will, but the decisions taken are not causally dependent in any deterministic manner. The person decides!

Contemporary Self

The account of the self has already moved beyond the various divisions into three, and that process will now be extended. There is the question of the emotions to be addressed, and to that is added the associated question of perception. In Chapter 1, perception was explicit in the exploration of the mind/body problem, and it seems sensible to include it explicitly in this present account.

Emotion and perception are akin to one another in the sense that each is to some degree visited upon us, not chosen by us. If we are sad or angry, then that is how we are, whether it is how we want to be or not, and although our decisions and actions may subsequently influence our emotions and lead to changes in them, they rarely control them. Our emotional states are what they are and there is little choice but to live with them – perhaps seeking to modify them – as best we can. The situation regarding perception is very similar. In part we can determine our perceptions, but only in part. In general, life from an experiential point of view is partly under control, the product of our own actions, but partly outside control, the product of nature or the actions of other people. So emotions and perceptions share the characteristic of being at least partially visited upon the individual. (With regard to terminology, the term 'experience' could be used in place of 'perception', but as it is sometimes said that a person experiences an emotion, 'perception' will be preferred. It can then be asserted that both perceptions and emotions are aspects of human experience.) Neither emotions nor perceptions can really be thought of as constituting parts of a person, however, not even in the 'so-to-speak' mode of the reason and conscience, but they do contribute to the totality of what an individual person is.

Before completing this rather convoluted account of the self, the question of memory needs to be addressed. It seems tempting to include memory as a 'so-to-speak' part of the being, to put it alongside the conscience and the will as a part or aspect of the being. But a closer analysis shows that this simply does not work. The reason is that memory suffuses the entire mental being in somewhat the same way that blood suffuses the entire physical body. Memory has therefore to be regarded as an all-pervading element of the personality. Whether it is will, conscience or appetite, nothing works for us unless it includes memory. A total loss of memory would leave us bereft of language and understanding, of recognition (of anything at all), and of any organized capacity for decision and action. We would be reduced to a merely vegetative state, and perhaps to even less than that. So without memory we would simply cease to be persons in any normally accepted sense. Memory is ubiquitous, and is not to be included as a part of a person, not even 'so-to-speak'.

Finally, there are two lesser but not insignificant points. It will be necessary on occasions to distinguish between the decision, taken by the will, and the interaction of mind and body that stems from it. In practice, if a person decides to raise the right arm, the decision and the interaction seem virtually indistinguishable, but conceptually they are not the same, and on occasions the distinction will be important. In terms of category, action at the mind/body interface stemming from a decision shares with perception and emotion the characteristic of being an exterior aspect of the self.

The second point brings the argument back to Plato and his notion of the appetite as the part of the self that embraces human physical desire. In recent times we have also become aware of the importance of instinct, chiefly as an imperative in the behaviour of animals, but not without significance for human beings. The intention is to use 'desire' as the encompassing title, writing separately of appetite and instinct when they are needed in context. This is not quite conventional usage, and is slightly awkward in that sense that 'desire', spanning appetite and instinct, will have to be distinguished from *thymotic* desire', spanning the endeavours of conscience and 'heart'. However, it will enable the argument to be kept reasonably close to the framework originally set by Plato.

How then does it all come together, in the non-systems way that belongs to the nature of a subjective being, and how does it relate to the physical and mental dualism that was explored in Chapter 1? It is convenient to use a table, even though the systems-type thinking is so commonplace that almost any tabular form is liable to be given a systems-type interpretation. In the table below, the behavioural characteristics of the self are shown in sequence, and proceed from acquisition, through cognition to volition. There are ten distinct elements:

ACQUISITION	COGNITION	VOLITION
Perception	Intellect |	Will
	| Reason	
Appetite |	Talent |	Action
| Desire		
Instinct |	Conscience |	
	| *Thymos*	
Emotion	'Heart' |	

It must be emphasized that the function of the table is to set the scene for subsequent discussion. It picks out and relates just those aspects of a human being upon which the argument will be chiefly focused. No other claim is entered for it! Memory is not shown explicitly – it is regarded as inclusive, covering virtually all the aspects that are separately identified. With regard to the sequential titles, 'acquisition' is not a particularly felicitous term, but no single word seems to be preferable. 'Reception' would have been an alternative, but it seemed to possess too many inappropriate overtones. 'Cognition' is simply the covering title for everything that happens between acquisition and volition. It needs to be added that acquisition and cognition, close as they are to our very being, remain in many ways the stuff of mystery. In particular, they have led to seemingly endless arguments by the chief protagonists of the mind/body dilemma. But they pale before the mystery of volition (or free will), which raises far greater problems, and requires a more thorough exploration.

In Chapter 1, the relationship of free will to scientific law was closely examined, and led to the adoption of the notion that reality is dual. At that stage, however, little detail could be offered concerning the actual operation of volition. With the table now available, it becomes possible to see a little further. Volition is the exercise of the free will, and spans both the will itself and the action at the mind/body interface that stems from it. How does volition come about? Evidently a person responds to the perception of events (external) and to the feel of emotions (internal), and is influenced in determining the response by the conjunction of appetite, instinct, reason, conscience and 'heart'. But the self or person is an autonomous being. His or her decisions are subject to a great variety of influences as indicated, but are actually made by the exercise of free will. This is crucial. In fact, it is only in this way that a conscious being can be identified authentically as a subject, and not found to be just another object, however complex.

Consider the question: how did a person make that particular decision? The inescapable answer is that it was done by the exercise of free will. All manner of influences may be identified. It may be that conscience says, 'Do this.' Desire says, 'Do that.' 'Heart' says, 'This is a time for timidity. Try doing nothing at all.' It may be that these influences are so powerful that reason is in danger of being elbowed out altogether. But the decision is nevertheless the decision of the whole person, influenced but not controlled by any of the individual aspects of his or her being. So ascribing the decision separately to the will, whilst helpful as a way of speaking and convenient in its consistency with the diagrams, is only ever 'so-to-speak'.

As remarked in Chapter 1, the question of free will has troubled both scientists and philosophers. The scientific answer is found in dualism, but the philosophic issue is subtler, and cannot be resolved by an appeal to ontological differences. The philosopher and mathematician, Martin Gardner, argues that free will is an impenetrable mystery, and believes that it simply has to be left as that.[3] Although his argument testifies to an acute level of difficulty, however, it need not deny us a further exploration. Free will is vitally important. Consider first the situation that would obtain if it did not exist. In its absence, the whole notion of moral responsibility – indeed responsibility of any kind – simply disintegrates. A person does what inner necessity requires him to do – responsibility is not the point! Furthermore, with the disappearance of responsibility, much of life as we comprehend it is reduced to myth. For example, the greater part of this book becomes mere nonsense. (Assuming that it is not nonsense anyway!) Not of course that it matters. I have no choice whatsoever about whether to write it or what to write in it. I simply write down whatever it is that my deterministic (or probabilistic) inner-self requires. Even more alarmingly, some unfortunate person may be obliged – also by inner necessity – to read what I have written, from one end to another. He may think that he can put the book down at any time that he chooses, but he deludes himself. Read he will, by inner necessity, even to the last syllable!

Even stranger is the notion of a deterministic being who thinks, deterministically, that he is not a deterministic being, but has the capacity for free choice. Could a deterministic being even form the concept of free choice? Probably not! The truth is that we have to hold on to the notion of free will. We believe that we possess free will, and to make sense of life we need to keep to that belief. It may be a mystery, but in a sense it is a mystery to which we know the answer. So if that is the case, what further positive points can be made about it?

Free will is of the very essence for a conscious responsible moral being. As an objection, according to the philosopher, William James, its unwarranted presence leads to situations in which the next action that a person undertakes cannot be linked causally to his previous state and experience.[4] In context, 'causally' seems to be understood in the scientific observational sense, relating to actions that could be predicted accurately given sufficient knowledge of previous circumstance. In other words, the absence of causality means that a person is not a system, and cannot have his or her actions explained by any reductive process. But suppose 'cause' is taken instead to mean that no other agency is involved, so that the decision and subsequent actions are only those of the autonomous person. Upon that interpretation, a person *is* linked causally to his or her decisions. Furthermore, the lack of inner necessity, in the first sense, does not disconnect the person from the previous self, nor does it require that a free act arrive *ex nihilo* and tack itself on to a person. On the contrary, a free act occurs by the internal decision (as distinct from internal necessity) of the person, and is influenced (but not determined) by the previous state of the person, in particular by reason, conscience, 'heart' and desire. Experience and emotion also play their part, but, however many influences are present, the decision is ultimately that of the autonomous human being.

That a person changes with each decision is undoubted, but that need not intrude upon the notion of continuing personhood. There is a danger of identifying a physical system in a somewhat idealized way. In practice, systems deteriorate or are made the subject of modification, so the advent of change puts an autonomous decision-making person at no greater risk of an identity crisis than a deterministic physical system. To be awkward about it, why should an autonomous decision, a free choice made from among a number of possibilities, be more difficult to accept than a necessity? Probably the answer lies in the triumphs of science and technology, successes that have limited the view of what is acceptable as a coherent step from one moment to the next. What we need to say is that existence includes both deterministic systems (and probabilistic systems) and autonomous decision taking persons. The former move by necessity (or probability) from one situation to another, the latter exercise choice among a number of possibilities. Both retain their coherence as they proceed from step to step.

Purpose and Value

These explorations of reality and human nature have so far stopped short of any consideration of purpose or value. In the first chapter, physical and mental reality was explored, and since then a closer look has been taken at the make-up of individual human beings. But what existence is for, and what is of value within it – nothing significant has yet been offered.

There have, nevertheless, been pointers. They appeared in the account of the *thymotic* aspects of a person, the conscience and 'heart', and also in the enquiring reason and the autonomous deciding will. Given that human beings have these sorts of characteristics, what is it that first emerges regarding purpose and value? Probably the need to be clear about the question! There is, or may be, a difference between some purpose that a person chooses for himself or herself, and a purpose that someone else, God perhaps, commends for that person. To make progress, the exploration starts with strictly human purposes, the purposes that individual human beings choose for themselves.

A mild but unavoidable point is that the purposes human beings choose do not have to be profound. Many of them arise straightforwardly from the ordinary exigencies of the day. From cleaning the teeth to mowing the lawn, from making coffee to washing dishes, life includes a whole range of activities, some routine, some not, that are simply based on immediate choice – and never mind the philosophy!

Moving only slowly beyond the kind of examples above, if human beings so choose they can live their lives almost entirely according to the pressures of appetite, instinct and emotion. It seems that the other creatures of this world live in this way (with or without emotion) because they hardly have any choice. The limited extent of their rational and *thymotic* development leaves them with just the combination of instinct and natural desire to tell them what to do. It may be that they have no choice at all, but it seems unnecessarily restrictive to discount reason and *thymos* entirely, at least for some animals. But that is not to suggest that reason and *thymos* among animals even begin to compare with those of human beings. What is assumed is that the higher levels of reason and *thymos* available to human beings offer them an altogether greater range of choices. But, as remarked, the choice can be made to live very largely according to appetite, instinct and emotion.

To complete the groundwork, of particular significance in any broader study of value and purpose will be the moral value of a person. Indeed, moral value is sometimes regarded as being synonymous with personal value itself, the entire value of a human being. It would be more accurate, however, to say that the value of a person is multifaceted, so that whilst moral value is normally included, a person could also be valued for wealth, power, individual talents or physical attributes. When speaking of value, particularly the value of a person, it is important to be as clear as possible just what form of value is under discussion.

Using the previous table of human aspects, it is evident that reason, conscience and 'heart' all contribute to the decisions of the human will, influencing the purposes that human beings set for themselves, and helping to determine the values, moral or otherwise, upon which choices are based. Where reason is dominant or at least significant, individual purposes and values fall under the span of personal philosophy. Following a fairly common practice, however, personal philosophy in this argument will normally exclude those purposes and values that relate specifically to organized religious belief and practice.

The next step in widening the horizons of value and purpose is to introduce the notion of ideology. For most people, human life is not just a matter of individual activity. It also involves participation in social life. The latter includes activities requiring loyalty to tribe, the making of commitments to the various groups and bodies to which individuals belong. Ideologies defining the values and purposes of the tribe are vitally important – and from now on the term 'tribe' will be used in a generic sense to mean any form of national or local social grouping.

Two points of immediate significance need to be noted. First, worldly issues of value and purpose do not exhaust the connotation of the terms, 'personal philosophy' and 'ideology'. There may also be a metaphysical content. (To avoid confusion, this will not extend to organized religion.) Secondly, the relating of individual and tribal values can be of critical importance. A person may have both a personal philosophy and a social or political ideology, and the two may not always deliver a consistent set of values. Sometimes they may be in outright conflict. Life can become complicated! These are issues that will be taken up in later chapters.

What is common to the values and purposes considered so far is that they are all essentially human, that is to say they are the values and purposes that human beings adopt for themselves. This limitation departs when consideration extends to religion. Still struggling to be clear about definitions, the term 'religion' will normally mean theistic religion, and often more narrowly than that, theistic religion in which God is believed in as the Creator of the world (universe). If something different is meant, then it will be stated. With regard to religion in its organized form, the organization can be one or both of two kinds. First, it can be an organization in the sense of an organized body of persons, and this may be an ecclesiastical hierarchy or a worshipping congregation. Secondly, it can be an organization of belief through a structure of doctrine – often expressed in holy writings or a creed. The two kinds of organization may come together in the form of structures and worshipping practices specifically intended to support doctrine. In this text these are the various senses in which the expression 'organized religion' will normally be understood. If a set of beliefs is being considered that belongs simply to a particular individual and does not necessarily conform to an organized religion, the preferred expressions will be 'personal religion' or 'personal philosophy'.

Within the framework of theistic belief, values and purposes are first and foremost those of God. Human purposes and values are not discounted, but are viewed in the context of what it is that God wills and what it is that he values. The consideration of values and purposes in these terms leads on to a further set of yet more searching questions. They begin at a fundamental level. What is the purpose of the world? What is the purpose of life? Answers sought on the understanding that God is the Creator tend to raise yet further issues concerning the origin of the world and of life within it. Origin, value and purpose form a trio of fundamental questions, all three of which can be seen as divinely determined, and beyond them is the ultimate question of human destiny. The beliefs of theistic religion normally include those that pertain to life after death – life eternal as it is put, the ultimate destiny of humankind.

In terms of strict rationality, there is nothing to prevent a person from believing in life after death without entertaining any kind of belief in a divine Creator. If one can arrive 'naturally' in this world without requiring divine activity, then arguably one might arrive in the next world by a similar natural process. Perhaps progress from this world to the next – even from earth to heaven – is just the way existence happens to be! Conversely, it is quite rational to believe in an eternal God, and yet to accept that life for human beings is limited to this world, to the single 'moment in annihilation's waste'. But whilst such possibilities are quite rational, in practice they find few adherents. It seems that the two beliefs, in God the Creator for our origin and in life after death for our destiny, have a strong tendency to be held in concert (or denied in concert). For the most part and for reasons to be discussed, this argument will proceed in accordance with the thrust toward dual belief (or dual disbelief).

Spirituality

To summarize, the issues of purpose, value, origin and destiny have been placed successively in the context of personal philosophy, ideology and religion. As the argument has advanced, so the range of purposes and values has changed and grown. This process now concludes by moving forward to the notion of spirituality. The study of personal philosophy, ideology and religion will continue, but the greater part of the ensuing text will be concerned with spirituality. This development will be facilitated by deliberately subsuming some aspects of personal philosophy, ideology and religion into spirituality, a process that will be rendered explicit later. The remainder of this chapter will be mainly concerned with establishing the structure of spirituality and marking out what will form the spiritual horizons.

Beginning with a geographical constraint, the intention is to focus chiefly upon spirituality in Britain. In addition, remarks about organized religion will usually be confined to the Christian religion. It is hoped, nevertheless, that substantial parts of the arguments concerning modern spirituality will have a wider application.

The tendency in Britain, arising out of its religious past, is to regard spiritual activity as being largely contained within the structures of organized religion. In a broad Christian sense, it relates to the more soulful aspects of religion, to prayer and worship, to Bible reading and the receiving of the sacraments. This assimilation of the spiritual within the religious derives from the strength of religious observance in the earlier history of the land. To offer a measurement, the England of the late middle ages contained separate Churches that were built for an average parish of less than a thousand people. From that time up to the early years of the nineteenth century, organized Christian religion continued to be a great and dominant force in the land, and the place of spirituality belonged manifestly within it. But then it all began to change. In the course of the next two hundred years, organized religion, measured numerically in proportion to the population, fell back progressively from its once majority state.

As this reduction in formal Christian belief and practice in Britain has been thoroughly charted, there is no requirement to dwell at any great length upon it. In recent times, a succinct account has been given by Don Cupitt in his book, *The Sea of Faith*.[5] As long ago as 1867, Matthew Arnold wrote of the 'long, withdrawing roar' of the 'sea of faith', and there has been time for a great deal more withdrawing since the middle of the nineteenth century.[6] No doubt historians will find a plethora of reasons for the change. Clearly, the industrial revolution and its associated social changes played significant parts in the process, and World War One, with its relentless and terrible suffering in trench warfare and its vast casualty lists, seemed to have hastened the change.

The second half of the twentieth century witnessed a significant further change. Schooldays in the 1950s included a religious assembly on a daily basis. During that period, for any young person attending Church on a regular basis, Saturday was the only day of the week which lacked a formal religious event. At that time, virtually everyone was 'C of E', unless he or she specifically claimed to be otherwise. Morality, particularly sexual morality, followed a formal and accepted pattern as prescribed by the Church. For example, heterosexual intercourse was believed to be sinful outside marriage, and homosexual and lesbian activities were sinful under any circumstances. Children were expected to be conceived, born, baptized and brought up, by two married parents. Death was to be followed by a Christian funeral service. Whilst people may not have always lived according to the Christian structures of behaviour and morality, they certainly knew what they were.

The funeral service excepted, remarkably little of that pattern of behaviour has survived into the beginning of the twenty-first century. Formal religious activity is virtually unknown for many young people. Sexual morality is utterly transformed. Allowing a vast generality, it appears that over about two centuries the acceptance of doctrine weakened first, and the decline in formal religious observance followed after a quite extensive period of time. Morality, once based upon religious belief, survived even longer in its conventional form, but finally gave way to different and secular moral codes.

What does all this mean for spirituality? Basically, if spiritual life continues to be thought of simply as an aspect of formal religious life, particularly the religious life of a person actively participant in the affairs of a denominational Church, then spirituality in Britain must have suffered a serious and protracted decline.

Central to the present argument, however, will be the belief that this definition of the spiritual is much too limiting. In a previous age, when participation in organized religion was almost universal, it was a limitation that did not register as a serious problem. Today, it is serious indeed! According to its dictionary definition, the spiritual is related to the spirit, the higher faculties and the soul, and it is incorporeal and ecclesiastical. Only in part is it necessarily religious. In an age when formal religious belief and practice are numerically at a low ebb, these other facets of spirituality will need to be separated from their previous religious associations if they are not to be denied much of their significance.

This notion was taken up by the religious writer Chris Scott, who put forward the possibility of what he called a 'secular spirituality'. To quote Scott: 'What I want to suggest is the possibility of a secular spirituality. This may sound like a contradiction in terms, but it is only so if one ties the concept of spirituality to a conventional religious belief system.'[7] Upon that understanding, secular spirituality in modern multicultural Britain encompasses the forms of spirituality that are located (or can be located) outside any of the principal religious organizations of the land. As such, secular spirituality is open to persons whose backgrounds belong to any or none of the great religious traditions. (To avoid a misleading impression, the focus upon secular spirituality is certainly not intended to question the religious spirituality of Christians active in their Churches. Nor does it question the spirituality of members of the other great religions in this now pluralist land. What is being addressed is the possibility of a spirituality arising outside the framework of religious bodies, and thus available to people irrespective of their formal religious beliefs or membership.)

The development of this secular approach will follow broadly the prompting given by the dictionary definition of the spiritual. Referring back to the table of the self, the relating of the spiritual to the 'higher faculties' points it toward the reason and the *thymos*, and their influence upon the will. There is a subtlety about the idea of the spiritual, however, and it will be important not to regard it simply as the aggregate of activities manifested separately in three different aspects of the person. As an example – and a critically important one – a secular spiritual activity should be viewed not as a moral activity in isolation but a moral activity arising from the conscience and undertaken in the context of the beliefs of the reason. It may be thought that this simply returns the spiritual to the religious, a moral activity enlightened by faith. That may be true in some particular cases, but what of the 'long withdrawing roar'? There is no escaping the fact that there is far less acceptance of religious doctrine than there used to be! Arguing in general terms, the spiritual, often in its secular form, embraces acts of will that stem from the conscience and 'heart', but acts that are chosen in the context of the beliefs and doubts with which the reason struggles. Organized religious beliefs may or may not be among them, or they may be present but the subject of fundamental doubt. To express the point in terms of values, spiritual values are moral values and values of the 'heart', but values that are examined and qualified by the reason, by its knowledge, beliefs and doubts. Finally, to pick up an earlier cautionary theme, it should be added that spirituality is always holistic, relating to the whole person, with the language of parts being only 'so-to-speak'.

The connotation of the term 'spiritual' is now going to be widened still further, and in two separate ways. In Chapter 1, the creative (or destructive) nature of decision-making was established. In the current chapter, both talent and intellect have been described as belonging within the compass of the reason. Building upon those foundations, the creative acts of the will that stem from the employment of talent will now be included within the realm of the spiritual. That is the first extension, one that will be returned to and explored in Chapter 8. The second, also involving the reason, extends the secular spiritual to include those activities that belong to the working out or implementing of ideologies. Clearly, these two extensions lead to a wider use of the term 'spiritual' than is commonly the case, but they remain consistent with the dictionary definition, and consistent too with the kind of argument that is being developed in this text, an argument that has chiefly to do with modern life in its secular setting.

The inclusion of ideology within the span of spirituality widens the argument by taking it into the field of political philosophy. Once again, the concern is chiefly with the way things are (and have been) in Britain, but it is appropriate at this juncture to widen the scope in order to look at political philosophy across Europe and beyond. The twentieth century has seen the rise and fall of the two political extremes of fascism and communism. It would be tempting to see the dramatic surge of extreme political ideologies as the counterpoint to the decline of religious belief, the 'long withdrawing roar of the sea of faith', but that would be both unfair and simplistic. Fascism and communism emerged out of centuries of secular political development, and were not disconnected from the social changes that accompanied the industrial revolution. That being said, stronger and more widely held religious beliefs – Christian religious beliefs – would almost certainly have intruded upon the progress of political extremism, whether of the left or the right. What is certain, however, is that during the twentieth century the human race came very close to universal domination (by force) first by fascism, in its most virulent form of nazism, and then by communism. Each in turn was largely thrust aside, and in the western world at least, political ideology has given way to something much more pragmatic, a mix of liberal democracy with the economics of free markets and the welfare state. The spiritual challenge that these occasion will be looked at in detail in Chapter 8. What needs remarking now is that the decline in formal religious belief and the growth of somewhat pragmatic thinking in politics, economics and social affairs have created a situation in which the significance of the spiritual, whether religious or secular, often seems less than clear.

Given this difficulty, it is important to try to be as exact as possible, even at risk of repetition. Spirituality belongs to the 'higher faculties' and is therefore to be identified among the activities of reason, conscience and 'heart'. With regard to reason, it will be discovered in both talent and intellect. Focusing upon the latter, it will arise chiefly in those thoughts that have to do with religious belief, personal philosophy or ideology. Until modern times, the religious content was dominant, but that has now fallen away, and for some people scarcely exists. Extreme political ideologies also emerged (and threatened) in the earlier years of the twentieth century, but they too have lost their place and influence. Political and social attitudes, certainly in this country but also in much of the western world, have moved towards pragmatism. The consequent danger for spiritual life is that it will lose its focus, and become identified (if at all) in ways that deny it a place in busy lives. In many cases the conscience will still be active, but not in ways that are understood to belong to a spiritual life. In consequence, the findings of conscience will be at risk of becoming incoherent, of losing out to other more dominant voices in the making of decisions and the exercise of free will. Whilst religious and political beliefs often continue to be held, they tend to be held but weakly, echoes perhaps of past enthusiasms, and as such are liable to exercise little influence upon the principal decisions of life.

What then can be said positively about the way forward for spiritual life? Some will hope for a religious revival – a resurgence of faith, so that reason issues forth in confident belief, and *thymos* is given a secure framework within which to work out its responses to the exigencies of life. Others will look for the day when the current political pragmatism will be superseded by something much more inspirational. A few may even think that a dramatic change in human spirituality will be brought about through a global war or other cataclysmic event. The way forward in this text, however, is less dramatic, at least as far as it is reasonable to look ahead. What is assumed is that much of spiritual life, hitherto located in organized religious belief and practice, will need to be relocated in secular life, however pragmatic much of that life may seem, or else lose its role in human affairs. The process of relocation can begin simply with the recognition that all human beings are creatures of reason, conscience and 'heart', and that it is possible for those elements of a human being to come together holistically to influence the will. Starting with that as foundation, the argument will proceed in the next chapter to the spiritual application of reason, and the grasp of truth that forms the first step in that endeavour.

Notes

1. Plato, *The Republic*, Book IV, c. 390 BC.

2. Francis Fukuyama, *The End of History and the Last Man*, Penguin Books, 1992.

3. Martin Gardner, 'The Mystery of Free Will', *The Night is Large*, Penguin Books, 1995.

4. William James, *Pragmatism*, 1907.

5. Don Cupitt, *The Sea of Faith*, SCM Press, 1986.

6. Matthew Arnold, '*Dover Beach*', 1867.

7. Chris Scott, *Between the Poles*, New Millennium, 1996, p. 4.

3

Truth and Doubt

Secular Spirituality and the Paucity of Knowledge

Historically, British spirituality was based almost wholly upon Christian religious beliefs. They were beliefs structured in bodies of doctrine and formally proclaimed by denominational Churches. If they constituted the established orthodoxy, they were strongly reinforced by the power of the state. That time has long gone. In today's multicultural society, many people are committed to religions other than Christianity. For others, almost certainly a majority in Britain, an early nurture in the Christian tradition has not been sustained into adult life. For those in the latter group, participation in religious activity has either reduced or even discontinued, at least where organized worship is concerned. As previously discussed in Chapter 2, for that group spirituality must either decline in correspondence or establish itself on a different basis. It is upon the second possibility that attention is now to be focused.

The exploration of modern spirituality in the previous chapter found a suitable starting point in the recognition that humankind is composed of conscious beings, endowed with reason, conscience and 'heart'. Looking first at reason, in the absence of formal religious beliefs, how could human beings apply their intellectual powers in ways that would be spiritually significant? In context, the expression 'spiritually significant' means significant in relation to fundamental questions of origin, destiny, value and purpose. One answer, or at least one approach to an answer, is to move the point of concern from the truth of an individual belief or proposition to concern for truth itself. This shift in the initial focus of spirituality can be summarized as follows:

Earlier religious spirituality began with *faith*.

Modern secular spirituality begins with *truth*.

These two contrasting statements constitute an oversimplification, particularly in the underlying assumption that spirituality divides tidily into the religious and the secular, but they can still serve as useful initial markers for the argument. Of course, a commitment to truth is hardly new!

'Wherever truth led, there I dared to follow.' These words, or strictly their Latin equivalent, were used as a first-person account of the philosophy of William Whiston, a liberal thinker and writer of the eighteenth century. Notwithstanding their venerable nature, however, they express in challenging form the first characteristic of modern spirituality, the commitment to follow truth irrespective of how uncomfortable the consequences might be. This is of course to regard spirituality in a positive sense. The calculated purveying of falsehood can also be an aspect of spirituality, albeit one that is warped and arid. Perhaps a better way forward is to lay the focus upon personal integrity. For many people today the beginnings of a spiritual approach to life is found not so much in the adoption of particular articles of belief as in the making of a commitment – a commitment to seek and uphold the truth, wherever it is found, even in the face of acute difficulty or danger.

Given the reference to the eighteenth century, the claim to modernity might appear overstated, but it seems nevertheless that the widespread grasp of the fundamental importance of objective truth is fairly recent. It has been evidenced particularly in the extraordinary growth in education that began in Victorian times with the building of elementary schools and gradually extended in the twentieth century to embrace a vast expansion of Universities and Colleges. In two hundred years from the beginning of the nineteenth century the educational scene has been utterly transformed. The concomitant awareness of the value of truth has become increasingly a characteristic of modern Britain, even though the previous grasp of faith – Christian religious faith – has fallen into numerical decline. Individual integrity, the commitment to truth, has gradually advanced, and in so doing has provided the first defining mark of modern spirituality. Furthermore, it is a form of spirituality that has developed primarily in secular society, although it would also be proper to acknowledge the vigorous encouragement that it has received from the more liberal elements of religious organizations.

Nevertheless, the claim to spiritual progress, evidenced in particular by the growth of education, will give an unrealistic sense of encouragement unless accompanied by a due recognition of just how difficult and demanding the pursuit of truth can be. This is a complex subject, but, without a serious attempt to spell out the problems, the earlier positive remarks about the growth of spirituality through the commitment to truth will stand as little more than platitudes.

To begin the exercise, problems emerge as soon as one moves from a merely intuitive idea of truth. The meaning of truth seems clear enough in ordinary usage, but its precise interpretation has been a long-standing source of contention. In recent times, however, the tendency has been to accept that truth is best accounted for by the notion of correspondence. A suitable starting point for this exploration, therefore, is the dictum that summarizes correspondence theory:

For something to be true it must correspond to the facts.[1]

The identification of the 'something' is important. There are a number of claimants, but for simplicity in this argument the role of truth-bearer will be limited just to beliefs and sentences. With regard to facts, knowledge of the facts comes in two kinds – the empirical and the *a priori*. Empirical knowledge derives from experience or introspection, but the *a priori* is obtained just from thought itself. It transpires that *a priori* factual knowledge is limited to the fields of mathematics, logic, and linguistic form. Anything else that is assumed to be true, *a priori*, is a belief rather than a known truth, and may therefore be in error.

At one stage, difficulties over empirical knowledge led philosophers of language to develop an alternative theory of truth – coherence theory.[2] It is a theory that derives from the fact that the only information available to us regarding an alleged empirical truth is that which our own experiences and introspection provide. We cannot get outside ourselves in order to check whether a particular sentence does or does not correspond with some external fact. The idea of coherence theory is that we test a sentence for truth, not by seeking correspondence with some external fact, but by checking the sentence and the experience that prompted it for coherence with other sentences and other experiences.

In recent times, however, the question of whether truth should be a matter of correspondence or coherence has been largely settled. What it comes to is that there are two questions to be resolved, not one. The first is – what do we mean by truth? The second – how do we discover truth? It is now generally accepted that what is meant by the truth of a sentence or belief is that it corresponds with the facts, and that the principal test for the truth of a sentence or belief is that it should cohere with other related sentences or beliefs.

This establishes, in outline, the general theory of truth. What happens when it used in practice? In particular, what happens when the empirical and the *a priori* come together? Beginning at the elemental or primitive level with the immediate raw experiences of life, it is commonly recognized that we make use of a variety of cognitive processes that are all based on unproven *a priori* assumptions. These cognitive processes, which include concept-forming, classification and recognition, are virtually instantaneous, often sub-conscious and effortless, and almost inescapable. For example, my recognition of a green and brown shape as a tree is not only immediate but usually of such intensity that any efforts that I make to set it aside are the subject of instant failure!

'Green and brown shape,' I tell myself, enthusiastically. 'Tree!' says an inner voice insistently, somewhere at the back of my mind. There is presumably some means of switching off this process of instant recognition, but I have yet to discover it.

The *a priori* presuppositions for these unavoidable sub-conscious interpretations are clearly the subject of belief. No matter how convincing they may seem, however, there is simply no way that they could provide the guarantees of assured belief that would result in their being impervious to error.

When we move from the physical to the personal, the distance between belief and knowledge increases. Virtually all the things that we believe about other people, their hopes, fears, joys, sorrows, attitudes and beliefs, are inferred from a combination of experience and introspection – and the bases of that inference are believed but not proved (or able to be proved).

Up to this point, the only *a priori* beliefs considered have been those that we hold sub-consciously and use in the immediate interpretation of everyday experience. If we press further, however, to explore knowledge and belief at the intellectual level, additional problems are swiftly encountered. In this context, 'intellectual' means anything that involves a person's reasoning powers and his or her consciously held beliefs. It is not limited to the scholastic. To fix the subject, there are three principal categories to be considered. They relate to everyday experiences, to science, and to revelation.

With regard to the first two, it is apparent that they are heavily dependent upon *a priori* assumptions that are neither proven nor susceptible of proof. Pride of place belongs to the principle of induction, without which science would be virtually non-existent and many everyday understandings would disappear. Induction takes a number of forms, the most widely used being the advance from the particular to the general, which can be stated as follows:

If something is found to be true in a number of observed cases, then it will probably be true in all similar cases.[3]

The principle itself is unproven. It is universally applied, however, and as the number of successful observed cases rises there is a powerful tendency to discount the 'probably' and treat the unproven general result as certain.

In close proximity to the principle of induction is found the principle of cause and effect. As discussed in Chapter 1, although the probabilities of Quantum Theory cause modern theoretical physicists to fret over the nature of causality, elsewhere the principle is widely applied. It figures both in everyday activity, and also in engineering and technology, where the results of science become plainly visible. As with induction, cause and effect constitutes an unproven principle, widely believed but lacking the certainty of knowledge.

Having established the paucity of underlying knowledge in everyday and scientific affairs, it remains to be asked what is the corresponding position with respect to revelation? In general, revelation is regarded as being either a miraculous or at least extraordinary public event, or an exceptional private experience or message, not directly available to others. In addition, and for some people, there are occasions when what is otherwise an ordinary event may approach the character of revelation.

The point about this final category is that an otherwise ordinary event becomes revelatory either because of the special significance of its content or because of a special interpretation given to it. A person sees the hand of God in a particular occurrence, or regards some conjunction of events as being more than coincidence. As written, this seems quite rational, but there is nevertheless a difficulty of terminology. The focus of human thought moves from the general principles of science to the miracles of religion without much pause to observe what happens in between. Excepting the term 'historical', the significance of the particularity of a non-miraculous event does not seem to have any conventional title by which it can be identified. In this text a title is desirable, but 'historical' will hardly suffice, as it carries very particular scholastic overtones. 'Interpretive revelation' is the choice, although not an altogether happy one as revelation by miracle or strictly private experience may also require an element of interpretation. The alternative would be to coin a word, but that would be an extreme measure. 'Interpretive revelation' it shall be, or 'revelation of the interpretive kind', with the intention of rendering the meaning explicit wherever possible.

In relation to the other aspects of knowledge, interpretive revelation is in some respects the most challenging. In large part, scientific exploration is concerned with the establishing of general principles. They are regarded as applicable to the physical universe, irrespective of any particular pattern or sequence of events. Thus the ability to repeat an experiment or to vary an experiment and obtain predicted results is seen as a principal goal of science. In contrast, revelation of the interpretive kind depends not on the repeatability of an event but upon its singularity and particularity. Significance attaches because of the particular nature of the happening. And because we live in a scientific and technological culture, there is a tendency to think that this focus upon the particular is somehow less compelling than the corresponding scientific focus upon the general.

To expand on this point, consider a teacher of a lesson on dynamics, using the blackboard to illustrate his talk about forces acting between a particle at point X and another particle at point Y. If a student points at the board and says that he is not sure that there are any particles at points X and Y, and asks what grounds there are for thinking there might be, the teacher would ordinarily assume that he was either being silly or deliberately mischievous. A blackboard demonstration using points X and Y is illustrative of the general, not the particular, and what is being exhibited is only an abstraction. This is a quite normal practice in teaching, and demonstrates a common acceptance of the value of general arguments.

But the burden of our observations is that the pattern of events is singular. This is inescapable, notwithstanding the fact that it is often overlooked. One interpretation of Quantum Theory is that there are many parallel universes spanning the myriad probabilities of quantum activity, but however imaginative and interesting such an idea may be it is also highly speculative. All that we are actually aware of is the singular progress of events in the one universe that we inhabit. Why then should we not look for a special significance in the fact that it is event A that has actually occurred, and not one out of events B to Z, any of which could have been described rationally, though fictionally, within the framework of scientific law? Differences between beliefs derived from scientific exploration and those from revelation, including interpretive revelation, should be regarded as being differences of origin rather than confidence. In particular, a reluctance to countenance the singularity of events as a possible basis for belief is simply to limit access to an inescapable feature of the evidential spectrum.

Before attempting to reach any further conclusions concerning revelation, two additional points need to be included in the argument. The first, which is virtually implicit, is that unlike common and scientific observation revelation is chiefly to do with religion. And the second point is that revelation, irrespective of its kind, is commonly and widely communicated by written text. The great religions have their sacred texts, and an important function of the texts is to convey the revelatory message of the religion. In consequence, a great deal of revelation is necessarily indirect. Persons living on this earth today saw neither the opening of the Red Sea nor the transforming of water into wine, but if they have read of them and believed what they read then the accounts become revelatory for them. This assertion needs a closer examination. Religious texts, texts that contain records of alleged occurrences of revelatory events, are open to common scrutiny. Their presence can therefore be described as part of everyday life, common experience, and not directly revelatory in content. But if a person believes the asserted written account of a revelatory event, it does seem to acquire a character that is beyond the merely ordinary. There is a problem in that recorded revelation is not very far removed conceptually from what has been called 'revelation of the interpretive kind'. To avoid possible confusion, the argument will proceed on the basis that there are three direct modes of revelation and one indirect, the indirect mode being the one that applies when a person believes and becomes committed to a revelation offered in recorded form.

With regard to distinguishing between knowledge and belief in revelation, the following outcomes can be noted. For a person who has had a direct revelatory experience, nothing less than a claim to be in receipt of knowledge is likely to be made. That being accepted, whilst an asserted revelation presented via the written or spoken word is also clearly open to belief, it unavoidably lacks the assuredness of knowledge.[4] Furthermore, because the events that constitute the substance of indirect recorded revelation are singular, any beliefs adopted in consequence will lack the capacity for potential support that is normally open to scientific belief through the agency of additional experiment and report. Whilst scientific evidence and theories are also normally held in recorded form, the records themselves are legion. For the outcome of any particular experiment or argument to be accepted and believed, therefore, it will have to stand the test of coherence. By its very nature, recorded revelation can only rarely face a similar test or enjoy a similar ground for support.

What then is the outcome of this survey of the principal means of acquiring knowledge and belief? The general thrust is plain enough. Knowledge, of whatever kind and however sought, is in very short supply. Our everyday experiences are understood and classified on the basis of unproven *a priori* assumptions. What we regard as the joys, sorrows, intentions and attitudes of others, can be obtained only by inference from experience and introspection, and the reliability of the inferential process is without guarantee. The greater part of science is based upon the principle of induction, the validity of which can only be assumed. Causality, triumphantly successful in technological application, is without proof as a principle upon which physical events depend. And since revelation is constituted by its very nature in singular events, when it is given indirectly through the written or spoken word it is unable to provide the certainty of knowledge.

Doubt and Diversity

The paucity of human knowledge has two major consequences. Firstly, beliefs have to coexist with doubts, and the doubts will be persistent. Indeed, they will be more than merely persistent, for many people they will occupy a place of fundamental importance in their lives. Secondly and equally importantly, not only will people come to believe far more than they know, but the variety of their beliefs will be vast. Furthermore, much of this variety of belief will be quite rational, stemming from different presuppositions rather than lapses in logic.[5]

At the strictly operational level, the context of limited knowledge, many beliefs and many doubts, does not present any great problem. Beliefs are formed, or at least working assumptions made, and put to use unless or until they fail. A certain scepticism prevails, but not of a kind that need deny anyone a base for the mechanics of everyday living. When a man approaches a closed door, for example, he simply acts to open it. He does not ordinarily dwell upon the uncertainties of the presuppositions that underlie his endeavours, nor does he reflect upon the philosophical question of whether the door enjoys an objective existence independently of being observed. He does not usually worry about the mind/body duality that comes into play in implementing his decision. He just opens the door, walks through and gets on with his life. And so it is with a host of daily activities that take up a very significant amount of our time. Knowledge may be in short supply, but that does not stop us making everyday assumptions and getting on with our lives!

A little surprisingly, perhaps, the situation in relation to much of science is no more difficult. Scientific principles and theories are sustained unless or until they are superseded as a consequence of more refined experiment or more comprehensive argument. Scientific beliefs are often therefore provisional in nature. Scientists regard much of their work as the modelling of reality, and are not unhappy to discard older less accurate models in favour of newer better ones, as and when the situation demands. Scepticism again prevails, but it is a cheerful sort of scepticism, a scepticism that any particular idea will endure, but an expectation that it will nevertheless play its part in the gradual refinement of ideas and the extension of understanding.

That comment marks out the boundary of the ready acceptance of doubt. Still on the subject of science, its cheerful acceptance of the limits of knowledge is applicable primarily to scientific endeavour in its operational modes, including particularly the applications of science to support technological development. As already shown in Chapter 1, difficulties arise quickly when attempts are made to advance our understanding at a fundamental level by applying scientific arguments to the great mysteries of the physical universe.

Scientific controversy, however interesting it may be, tends to be esoteric in nature. More immediate, widespread and intensive are the problems that occur at the behavioural level, and this applies particularly where there are moral issues concerned. Where there was once a common understanding of morality, based upon biblical teachings, today the lack of certainty and the choice of quite different presuppositions obtrude heavily upon the morality of social and sexual behaviour, and upon attitudes to work and to wealth.

Nor do the problems stop with differing beliefs about personal behaviour. Political beliefs are also many and varied, and, given the shortage of knowledge and the prevalence of doubt, suspicions are particularly manifest in a sceptical Britain about any claim to a political ideology. It is also evident that, in the modern world, the principal religions will find themselves obliged to struggle with the issues of doubt and the presence of a multiplicity of beliefs. It transpires therefore that the choice of the commitment to truth as the first element of modern spirituality brings with it the immediate problems of doubt and diverse belief, and these can invade our morality, our political perceptions and our religious understandings. A commitment to truth may seem intuitively sound, even obvious, but its ramifications are many and often less than comfortable! With the commitment to truth comes the acceptance of doubt, and doubt can be very painful.

Paradox

The problems associated with truth are of two quite different kinds. The ones already explored – the problems of doubt and diversity of belief – are problems that are consequential upon people choosing the commitment to truth as the first characteristic of their spiritual lives. Often people would not overtly relate a commitment to truth to the composition of their spiritual lives, but that is effectively how it is! The second kind of problem is that which occurs in and hinders the actual implementation of truth.

The first of these arises from the actual definition of 'truth', and the logical processes that are used to discern truth in an argument. This is a problem that is largely of a scholastic nature, but it is not rendered unimportant thereby. It is given expression in what are described as the semantic paradoxes, of which Epimenides' paradox, or the Liar paradox as it is otherwise known, is the most celebrated.[6] Arguments that relate to the paradoxes are lengthy and complicated. Only an outline will follow, with references given to more detailed accounts, and the conclusions offered in the final paragraph of this section.

The discussion that follows will centre chiefly on the single example of the Liar paradox. Expressed in its simplest form, the paradox can be demonstrated with the self-referring sentence:

(a)   Sentence (a) is false.

Consider the following. If sentence (a) is true, then it is true that sentence (a) is false, in which case sentence (a) is false. On the other hand, if sentence (a) is false, then it is not true that sentence (a) is false, in which case sentence (a) is true. Confusing? To an extent, but surprising that it has been confusing enough to have caused problems for philosophers and logicians for more than two thousand years!

Does it matter? To a degree, yes! How can we be confident about discerning truth in an argument if the normal processes of logic can apparently render the same sentence both true and false? A partial answer is that strange results of this kind only occur in certain well-known cases, and these are usually cases that include an element of self-reference. If a means can be found to take out the self-reference or its equivalent, then the problem will go away! It is only a partial answer, however, as it turns out that there are occasions when we do want to use self-reference in an argument, or at least something very close to self-reference.

About a hundred years ago, the mathematician and philosopher Bertrand Russell identified a paradox in mathematics roughly corresponding to the Liar paradox of ordinary language.[7] It is called Russell's set paradox, and its discovery put a question mark against the very foundations of mathematics. Russell prescribed a solution, both for his own and for the Liar paradox (and for all the others) in what he termed the Theory of Types. Very briefly, if a person, John say, talks about the world, his sentences are of a particular type, but if he talks about the sentences that talk about the world, then what he says is of one type higher. And if he talks about the sentences that talk about the sentences that talk about the world, then his talk is one type higher still! By avoiding mixing the types of sentence, self-reference is also avoided, and the paradoxes are removed. Russell's argument has been analysed and often criticized – certainly the constraints involved in refusing to mix the types have created other logical difficulties. Nevertheless, the Theory of Types does provide comprehensive grounds for the dismissal of self-reference, and many of the solutions for the paradoxes that have been propounded more recently are at least distant cousins of that theory.

In this text, a further answer to the Liar paradox is offered, but in order to reach it a brief digression is needed. Sentence (a) is one of a pair of sentences that do no more than declare their own truth-values. The other is the sentence:

(b)   Sentence (b) is true.

Unlike (a) and its variations, upon which so much energy has been expended, sentence (b) has attracted virtually no attention, presumably because no contradiction stems from its assumption. But consider the question whether or not (b) is actually true or false.

According to correspondence theory, a true sentence corresponds to the facts. But what is the situation with the sentence that declares only of itself that it is true. The answer is not obvious. Assume the sentence to be true and the fact to which it corresponds is the truth that has been assumed. Assume it to be false and the fact to which it fails to correspond is the falsehood that has been assumed. Neither seem to be genuine facts, so which is it? The answer is that the sentence could equally well be either true or false, the reason residing in the absence of any substantive relevant fact against which the sentence can be tested for correspondence.

Two possible ways forward can be identified. The first is to accept that sentence (b) has no truth-value, which would entail the acceptance of a truth-gap logic. This approach has been explored by Kripke, and is based on the argument that the sentence is not grounded, that is to say its truth-value does not depend on the truth-value of any sentence that excludes the concept of truth.[8] His solution involves the loss of the law of the excluded middle in its normal form, a solution that sits uncomfortably alongside the standard framework of logic.

The alternative is to cleave to the law of the excluded middle, and to treat what has been called sentence (b) as being not properly a declarative sentence at all. This treatment would be justified by the absence of any substantive relevant fact against which the sentence could be tested for correspondence. Although what is called sentence (b) appears to be satisfactory, the sequence of words would then be understood as belonging in the same camp as:

(c) This elephant is true.

The claim of impropriety in case (b) is sustainable only because (b) is self-referring. What is important is that a similar argument is applicable to (a), the supposed sentence that says only of itself that it is not true. Like (b), it either belongs to a truth-gap logic and has no truth-value, or it has to be treated as not being a genuine declarative sentence at all.

In putting forward this second option, the benefit is claimed of appealing to a common understanding of truth, as expressed through the idea of correspondence. In practice, it is very close to Kripke's position, but avoids the complication of introducing a logic with truth-gaps. Instead it removes the Liar paradox by refusing to admit its generator as a genuine sentence. It is also a process that leaves open the question of the extent to which self-reference can still be legitimately used.

In summary, many different solutions to the paradoxes have been advanced, but their use tends to constrain other desirable forms of argument, and they are therefore to be applied as sparingly as possible. That being said, the difficulties that arise with the paradoxes are for the most part ones that can safely be left to the logicians. What does need to be held in mind, however, is that the most common source of such problems is the use of self-reference. If self-reference is found to be a desirable element in an argument, then care needs to be taken lest it be used in ways that also admit paradoxical conclusions.

Belief and Commitment

Scholastic problems are not the only ones that hinder the search for truth. Moving from the scholastic to the political and social, it is quickly apparent that not everything in Britain conspires to support the cause of the disinterested enquiry after truth. Truth is described as the first casualty of war, and wars have been plentiful in the twentieth century and may be prominent in the twenty-first. Subterfuge, deceit, propaganda, all these play an inevitable and sometimes praiseworthy part in armed conflict. A spiritual commitment to truth cannot be observed without question when issues of life and death, for individuals and whole communities, may be at stake.

In our legal system, the adversarial method practised so intensely in courts of law runs the risk of the pursuit of truth becoming subordinate to the task of winning the case. Politics shows a similar characteristic, where winning the vote may seem of overriding importance, and of course free-market economics can introduce powerful inducements to be less than strictly accurate in advertising utterances. This is not to criticize adversarial and competitive systems in general, but it is to remark that truth is not a natural beneficiary!

So the honest espousal of what one believes to be true, irrespective of its nature, is not always easy in modern society. Education and the widespread acceptance of scientific method are encouragements to truth, and this can apply whether the subject relates to ordinary daily life or to fundamental belief. But there are social pressures that drive in the opposite direction, and are not easily put aside. In Britain today, the life of Mr Valiant-for-Truth may not be at risk, but there will be subtler pressures against which he will have constantly to strive.

In identifying the ideas of secular spirituality and advancing the commitment to truth as its first characteristic, a minor host of terms and expressions have been used. The ideas expressed in terms of 'purpose', 'value', 'origin' and 'destiny', were the initiators of an exploration that embraced personal philosophy, ideology and organized religion, before reaching out finally to spirituality itself. In all of this, the importance of belief has been implicit from the beginning. It is now evident that a similar level of importance needs to be attached to the associated concept of commitment. Belief and commitment belong in each of personal philosophy, ideology, religion and spirituality. They are always closely interrelated, but there are times when they also need to be distinguished from each other, lest the thrust toward them drift into confusion.

Introspectively, a person uses reason to recognize that he or she possesses both a reason and a conscience. Likewise, a person may use conscience to make a commitment to apply reason to conscience and to exercise integrity. Reason and conscience are thus linked at the very beginning of spiritual life. (Logically the argument seems to follow a very tight loop!) Belief without commitment is narrowly intellectual, not spiritual, but commitment can rarely be formed without belief. Often beliefs and commitments – the contents of reason and conscience – are so closely intertwined as to be scarcely distinguishable, and the language relating to them becomes merged. That is not a problem, providing that it is recognized as occurring, so that the distinction can be identified if required. Exploring further, commitments may be formed in respect of any or all of the various aspects of personality identified as appetite, reason, conscience and 'heart'. Excepting the first, belief will often be needed as a precursor to the forming of commitments. Furthermore, where beliefs are required, the truth of those beliefs will be of great importance!

What is the status of that last remark? In the context of the Theory of Types, it is a second order statement, a belief about beliefs, a belief about the importance and value of a belief being true. It leads on to the second order commitment to form beliefs only with integrity, to seek diligently for the truth. Whether this second order process actually begins with reason or conscience is less clear. Perhaps it needs to remain unclear, as reason and conscience should only be regarded as parts of the person in a 'so-to-speak' manner. What matters is the recognition that spiritual life may begin in this way, with reason and conscience coming together to grasp the spiritual value of things being true and to influence the will in forming the commitment to the pursuit of truth.

That is sound as far as it goes, but in a sense it is still the easy part. What must be done next is to proceed from (second order) musing about truth to exploring those specific beliefs and commitments (of the first order) to which the (second order) commitment to truth could apply. Those are the beliefs and commitments that constitute the principal elements of modern spirituality, and they form the subject matter of the greater part of the ensuing text.

Finally and emphatically, in exploring specific beliefs and commitments, it is necessary to accept the persistence of doubt. The more closely we analyse our knowledge of the facts, the smaller it turns out to be. Uncertainty is the human lot! The more determinedly we seek the truth, the more often we are obliged to acknowledge just how limited is our capacity to find it.

Notes

1. Correspondence Theory. 'For something to be true it must correspond with the facts' is a distillation of a number of statements embodying very much the same notion. For a comprehensive treatment of the subject see D. J. O'Connor, *The Correspondence Theory of Truth*, Hutchinson, 1975.

2. Coherence. The use of coherence as a test for truth can be exemplified as follows. If John says, 'I am in pain', the fact of his being in pain is immediately available to him, so that the truth of the sentence is both established and assured. It is for him a known truth. If he says, 'I have had a visual experience which I interpret as the cat sitting on the mat', a similar situation arises. Once again the sentence is for him a known truth. But if he just says, 'The cat sat on the mat', the situation is different. The fact to which the sentence must correspond if true is out there in the world, objectively real, not simply a part of his experience. But the experience is all that John has, and that may be in error. He may be dreaming, or suffering from hallucination, or misapprehending in some other way. What he does therefore is check the sentence and the experience that prompted it, against other relevant sentences and experiences. If they cohere, then he regards the sentence as being true. If that seems a little weak as a test for truth, it should be noted firstly that it is what everybody does practically all the time, and that secondly, 'there is no alternative'!

3. Induction. The principle of induction is normally introduced in terms of the step (the inductive leap) from an initial set of given results to one asserted addition. A general result follows in which the step is taken from an initial set of results to a more general asserted addition. It is the latter that is indicated in the main text. In none of its manifestations is induction proven, and the widely accepted notion that inductive probability approaches certainty as the number of known

results increases is purely intuitive. Attempts to give an analytic account of the process of induction have failed. In the present text, it is argued that the reason for this failure lies in the fact that induction is essentially creative, and that creativity does not fall within the boundary of systematic process.

4. Written or Spoken Word. The point relating to revelation is part of a more general argument. If Tom sees what he thinks is a tree, he may be mistaken in his interpretation, but he is not mistaken about having an experience (of a green and brown shape). Strictly, Tom knows that he has had an experience, and believes that he has seen a tree. If Tom tells Harry that he has seen a tree, all Harry can know for certain is that he has received a spoken message. He cannot be sure that the message is true, he cannot even be sure that Tom has delivered it – the experience may just be a dream. So all that we know from the spoken or written word is the message. Its origin and validity are without guarantee. This applies to recorded revelation, as much as to any other kind of information.

5. Rationality and Irrationality. Beliefs do not become irrational simply because they are not assured. To be irrational, a belief must either contradict some other belief that is also being maintained – strictly speaking it is the combination of beliefs that is irrational – or must fly in the face of some widely accepted though unproven principle of existence. The second is a weaker form of irrationality, but not unimportant in a society prone to adopt general principles. With those exceptions, however, it is not irrational to hold beliefs in the absence of comprehensive relevant knowledge of the facts. For example, the only necessary condition for an inductive conclusion is that it does not contradict any of its premises. Nothing more is required. So it is not a criticism to assert that people believe more than they know, simply a statement of how things are. Similar arguments can be adduced for doubts. They too can often be held without any departure from rationality. Different people can hold different beliefs and different doubts, with no loss of rationality, except under one of the precise conditions described above.

6. Epimenides' Paradox. Epimenides, a Cretan from Cnossus, of about the sixth century BC, is credited with asserting that Cretans never tell the truth. Thus he instituted the paradox that bears his name. In modern dress it is offered as the Liar paradox, and has probably generated more discussion (and confusion) than any other paradox.

7. Bertrand Russell. For a detailed study of Russell's set paradox and the Theory of Types, see Whitehead and Russell, *Principia Mathematica*, 1910, Cambridge University Press, reissued 1967.

8. Saul Kripke, 'Outline of a theory of truth', contained in *Recent Essays on Truth and the Liar Paradox*, Clarendon Press, 1984.

4

God and Eternity

Sources of Belief

With much made in previous chapters of the decline in formal religious belief and the possibility of a secular spirituality, it may seem surprising to return so swiftly to what are inescapably religious matters. In explanation, it was never intended to depart from a spirituality that was wholly religious, only to become immersed in one that denied any religious content whatsoever. Whilst serious doubts pertain to theism, there are also serious doubts pertaining to atheism. The intention in this chapter is to explore and develop ideas in the context of religious uncertainty rather than unreligious certainty. As before, when writing of beliefs and doubts, attention will focus chiefly upon the circumstances in Britain and the doctrines of the Christian religion, although it is hoped that the argument and outcomes may be of wider interest.

Christian religious beliefs derive from three principal sources. First there is the Bible, secondly the associated teachings of the Church, and thirdly what is termed 'natural theology'. Beliefs are also powerfully influenced by emotions and by the *thymotic* elements of life, particularly those of morality and love. From the interplay of these sources and influences emerge the religious beliefs of individual human beings. (This part of the argument is deliberately simplified by its restriction to persons with a Christian religious background. Clearly, the sources, if not the influences, would change profoundly for persons with a non-Christian background.) The message of the Bible is revelatory in character, recorded revelation to use the previous description, and the principal doctrines of the Church derive from it. In contrast, natural theology grows out of common and scientific observation, and is formed today with the aid of scientific modes of thought. In combination, these constitute the source materials of belief, whilst the emotions and *thymos* provide the principal internal factors responsible for qualifying the beliefs, or sometimes even abandoning them.

Chapter 2 contained an outline of the reduction in Christian religious belief from its high orthodox plateau two centuries ago to the present state of widespread doubt and unbelief. Examining the contemporary scene at somewhat closer range, it is evident particularly among younger people that the numbers engaged in religious worshipping practice are greatly diminished. What is also clear is that the social conventions of family life, once so firmly grounded in Christian teaching, are now inclined to float free from any kind of anchoring. Nevertheless, although less than 10 per cent are now regular churchgoers, the results of the 2001 census reveal that just over 70 per cent of people in the United Kingdom still describe themselves as Christian. Much less clear is what the Christian non-churchgoers actually believe, or, equally to the point, what they no longer believe. In trying to find an answer, what emerges as a significant part of the problem is the acute reluctance of people, particularly the English, to engage in any kind of religious discourse. Evidence is anecdotal, but it does seem that this constraint upon religious discussion applies particularly strongly in those areas where traditional beliefs or religious conventions are thought to apply. Of course, this reluctance is explained to some considerable extent by the very creditable determination on the part of the English to respect the privacy of others with regard to their differing religious beliefs. But it does have its drawbacks, especially when one is trying to write intelligently about contemporary belief and observance!

One widespread consequence of this reluctance to explore religious belief, or to admit to its absence, is that all kinds of excuses are produced to explain a lack of participation in Church services. The language of the service is held to be old fashioned and obscure, or else it is 'happy-clappy' and lacking in dignity. Hymns are too ancient or too modern. The congregation is allegedly unfriendly, husband works late on Saturday nights, younger son has to be taken to football training on Sunday mornings, there is no other convenient time to do the shopping, and so on and so on. Everything and anything is on offer other than the straightforward and obvious statement that one does not believe what the Church proclaims! But whilst this legion of reason and excuse undoubtedly has some validity, it must nevertheless be presumed that it is the outright absence of belief, or at least an absence of some beliefs, that stands as the principal reason for the corresponding absence of a large part of the British population from the pew. Assuming that is indeed the case, what is it that has happened in respect of beliefs, doubts and disbeliefs?

For convenience of argument, the issues of religious belief, doubt or disbelief will be divided into those relating to God and Jesus, and those concerning the human race and its destiny. A fundamental religious question for human beings is whether this brief life on earth is the whole of personal existence, or whether there is to be life after death, or life eternal as it is more expansively expressed. As remarked in Chapter 2, although there is nothing irrational about believing separately in God or in life after death, neither of these singular positions finds many adherents. For the most part, people either believe both in God the Creator and in life eternal, or in neither. Similarly with regard to doubt, it either encompasses both beliefs, or it touches neither. As will be discussed later, there are substantial reasons for this being so, and in consequence the thrust toward dual belief or dual disbelief will normally be accepted.

Another more intellectual point concerns beliefs in God that differ from the belief in God as Creator. There are some very thoughtful people who hold positive but alternative beliefs, beliefs that are neither atheistic nor agnostic, so that they still believe in God, but believe differently. As the positing of alternative beliefs provides considerable scope for confusion, let it be stated firmly that in this text the interpretation of the word 'God' will normally be 'Maker of heaven and earth' as the Apostles' Creed puts it. If a different meaning is intended, then it will be declared. An exploration of some of these alternative ideas is offered in the final section of this chapter.

Proceeding with the principal argument, the central Christian question concerns the beliefs people hold about Jesus, and the way those beliefs relate to the ideas of God and eternity. The elementary notion, based for many people upon doctrines first learnt at school or Sunday school, is the one given vivid expression by Cecil Frances Alexander. In her well-known hymn, *There is a green hill far away*, Jesus is described as the one who, by his crucifixion, 'pays the price of sin'.[1] The encompassing idea is that of a divine drama, in which God responds to human sin by closing the door to heaven, and Jesus by his sacrifice opens it again, or persuades God to open it. Some members of the human race, or perhaps the whole of the human race, the numbers depending on the particular variation of the belief, are then permitted to enter. That in very simple terms is the putative doctrine. Judging from the widespread absence of persons from the Christian pew, it is also the doctrine that has in so many cases been set aside. What does not depart, however, is respect for the person and actions of Jesus. In nearly all cases, this still remains clearly in place. Furthermore, the moral and other teachings of Jesus continue to be held in very high regard, even where there is a marked reluctance to implement them.

It may be argued that this notion of Jesus and his sacrifice is more rudimentary than elementary. But for many people living today in an almost wholly secular society not much more is likely to be available. Rudimentary it may be, but this is the kind of belief that people acquired, or at least learnt something about in early youth, and it thus becomes the form of belief that is liable to be set aside in later years. Of course, the argument is very limited and leaves open a whole range of questions relating to alternative or more developed forms of Christian doctrine, including particularly those of a modernist or liberal nature. They will be returned to later. For the present, the intention is to remain focused upon the withdrawn position in which so many of the people of Britain seem currently to reside.

In terms of the departure from belief, it is not difficult to pick out the general pattern. Beliefs that depend chiefly upon revelation, the beliefs derived from Bible and Church, are those that are most likely to have been given up. Modern fashions of thought, the evident triumphs of science through technology, the search for objective truth, all these make it difficult to sustain beliefs based largely upon records of a distant revelation. Furthermore, modern morality calls into question the damnatory elements of earlier doctrine.

Bereft of their previous revelatory structure, what happens to the individual beliefs in Jesus, God and life after death? As remarked, the attitude toward Jesus tends to be sustained at the level of respect, often very deep respect, for his teachings and his example. The belief in his divinity becomes more problematic, however, as associated beliefs diminish. With regard to beliefs in God and in eternal life, with revelation less dominant their continuation becomes increasingly dependent upon the acceptance of a modern natural theology.

How does that work? There is no single answer, but what could be termed the cosmological reason is well to the fore. For many people, the idea that the universe could somehow have been self-generating seems unsatisfactory. But if the universe was created, it must have had a creator. How was the creator created? No answer is needed to that question because the creator is the Creator, the Divine Being, the Almighty God, the One who is beyond time and space and human understanding. Some philosophers fret, but this kind of answer is meaningful for many people, and attempts to derail it with logical argument seem to put more upon the foundations of logic than they can actually sustain.

The cosmological argument leading to belief in God the Creator operates chiefly at the common sense level. Cosmology as a modern science is not essential. Belief is straightforwardly available upon a modest application of reason. It is worth adding, however, that when the science of cosmology is invoked it leads to an uncertain conclusion. Belief in God the Creator is encouraged in some ways but not in others. According to modern scientific studies, the universe possesses a number of quite distinct and precise properties, without which the emergence of human beings as intelligent observers would apparently not have been possible. According to some scientists, the presence of these precisely formed properties points to a Creator who specifically designed his creation so that intelligent life would be bound to emerge. There is, however, an alternative view that posits the universe that we inhabit as just one among a myriad of parallel universes, all with differing properties. Unsurprisingly, the universe that just happens to have the correct set of properties to enable us to emerge is the one that we are busy observing! There is nothing special about it, and no need for a Creator specifically for our universe. Arguing yet further, an application of Occam's razor would seem liable to cut out this myriad of postulated universes in favour of the greater economy of a single universe and a divine Creator. But then again, perhaps economy is not the most important principle. The argument continues, with pointers being constructed in each direction, but nothing available in the way of proof.[2]

Beyond the analytic arguments, however, belief in God the Creator is strongly reinforced by the existence of our own human creativity. At least in the western world, we live virtually the whole of our lives, literally from birth to death, in the immediate presence of human artefacts. Clothes, houses, furniture, domestic and office equipment, motor vehicles and other forms of transport, these are with us at all times. Naturists sitting in a field or swimming in a river are about the only examples straightforwardly available of persons wholly separated from the things that humans make! So our lives are continuously intertwined with the objects of our own creation, and life would be utterly different without them. Of course, we create chiefly out of raw material, not *ex nihilo*, but nevertheless we do create and the process of creation, the capacity to create, is basic to our nature. When we contemplate the origins of our universe, it is quite natural for us to think in creative terms, of God the Supreme Being as God the Creator. But that of course is still only one side of the argument. What in a previous age were thought of as the proofs of God's existence are now recognized to fail. Both science and our own creativity may encourage us to believe in God the Creator, but they cannot prove that we are right.

How does one plot a path through all this? Whilst there are many different beliefs and doubts prevalent in modern society, some held more reasonably than others, the problems concerning the revelatory nature of the Bible do seem of particular significance. In a scientific age, this is partly due to a scepticism about revelation generally, but it is much more because of the difficulty of translating revelation (or anything else) from one age and mindset to another. To give examples, the mediaeval world looked up at the sun, the moon and the stars, wondered about them, and concluded that it must be the angels that kept them upon their appointed paths. So the combination of common observation and worldview supported the biblical accounts of the presence of the angelic host. Today, in a gravitational universe, no such support is forthcoming. In corresponding fashion, the ancient (and not so ancient) world, believed that human characteristics were inherited solely from the male 'seed', with the female limited to the role of 'mother earth'. Given that understanding, the virgin birth of Jesus was effective in protecting him from the inheritance of original sin. The discovery of the human female egg in the eighteenth century deprived the biblical account of that particular significance. In general, changes in worldview do not actually prove or disprove anything, but they do encourage caution in the uncritical acceptance of biblical texts, or of the early orthodoxies of the Church. Doctrines need to be understood in the context in which they were generated, and only with great care translated elsewhere. In consequence, it is more straightforward today to believe in Jesus of Nazareth in ways that emphasize his role as teacher and exemplar, than it is to sustain the traditional beliefs formulated by the early Church. Clearly, these are somewhat fragmentary remarks and they raise more questions than they answer, but it is sufficient at this stage simply to recognize that it is beliefs linked to revelation that are particularly prone to difficulty. (Specific questions relating to belief in Jesus and the biblical records will be left deliberately incomplete in this chapter, but they will be returned to in greater detail in Chapters 7 and 9.)

Although the problems of revelation occasion both doubts and disbeliefs, when it comes to natural theology the idea that the universe was created by God does seem to command a greater confidence than the notion that it just happened. Human decision-making is creative (or destructive) in the physical world, and human decision-making belongs to and is dependent upon the presence of ourselves as mental or spiritual beings. Extrapolating from that perception, it seems more convincing to think of the world and ourselves within it as created by God, than to imagine that it was somehow the outcome of an uncreated quantum fluctuation. If the idea of a quantum fluctuation underlies the explanation by the cosmologist of the origin of existence, then it is reasonable to think that someone somehow must have taken the decision that there should be a quantum fluctuation! Of course, it cannot be proved. For many people, it remains a matter of cautious belief, tinged with doubt!

An Interesting Universe

In pressing forward, it is reiterated that the evidence of everyday life as well as scientific study is multifaceted. In part it supports belief in God and eternity, in part it is antipathetic to such beliefs. Perhaps of even greater significance is the fact that much of what is observed turns out to be vague or even ambiguous from a believing standpoint. In addition, the *thymotic* content of our lives, our sense of morality and commitments to compassion and caring, they too can be variable in their effects, in some cases assisting religious belief, and in others doing the opposite. For many people, the writer included, the outcome is one of fundamental and sustained uncertainty. We do not know that God is present, but, equally, we do not know that he is not. We cannot be sure that there is any further life that succeeds this life, but neither can we be sure that there is not. Uncertainty is our lot!

Furthermore uncertainty cannot be ignored. If John was certain that his house would not burn down, then he would not need to insure against fire. But he is not certain, so he does! Equally, if an insurance company knew that his house would burn down, then it would refuse to insure him. But it is not certain, so it does! The essence of the whole vast insurance industry is uncertainty, not just plain ignorance. Uncertainty is incorporate in our lives and is not to be brushed aside, or treated as a common excuse for doing nothing. In particular, uncertainty as to whether the universe has a creator is not a good reason for setting the possibility aside. Uncertainty about theism is not a sufficient ground for the adoption of atheism.

Given the uncertainty, it is intended to examine the questions of God and eternity, not from the stance of a fervent believer, but from that of doubting believer and earnest enquirer. A belief in God the Creator will be adopted as a working presupposition, in order to see where modern thinking and modern knowledge can take it.

The assumption being made, the exploration begins with that icon of modernity, the computer game. Observing young people engaged in active real-time games (often violent on the screen), it is quickly evident that the activity is only interesting because the complexity and speed of the machine render its responses sophisticated and uncertain in the eyes of the participants. If the games' player knew in precise detail exactly what the machine would do, and could match the speed of the machine in doing it, interest would very swiftly pall. But if that is true for a young man and the virtual reality of his computer game, does not a corresponding argument apply to the omnipotent and omniscient Creator and the actual reality of his created universe? To put it simply, would not a Creator, with a detailed knowledge of every circumstance and event, from everlasting to everlasting, find eternity to be an eternity of boredom? Given the obvious answer to the rhetorical question, what could be done to rescue the situation? A possible solution would be to inhabit the physical universe with autonomous spiritual beings, genuinely able to form their own beliefs, make their own decisions, and live their own lives. That would be a quite different matter, as it would involve the uncertainty and freshness of relationships between truly independent spiritual beings.

Such a notion, of course, is more than mere speculation. There is a distinct echo of the earlier study concerning physical and mental existence. According to that argument, the physical universe is the subject of deterministic or probabilistic closure, except where it interacts with mental beings. Were we to exclude such intervention, then God would know the whole activity of the physical universe, from its birth in the 'big bang' to its decline into ultimate stasis, either exactly or at least in terms of probabilities. Such a universe would lack purpose and interest, it would not be fulfilling to its creator. But the previous argument spoke also of subjective beings, human beings, inhabiting a mental realm in which there are no scientific laws of either a deterministic or probabilistic kind. In their place is freedom, so that mental beings are able to make their own judgements and decisions, act responsibly (or irresponsibly), and be creative in their own right, through their interaction with the physical world. According to the argument for dualism in Chapter 1, that is how the world is and how individuals are related to it and able to act within it. Clearly such a combination of physical objects and mental beings would correspond positively and directly with the concept of an interesting created universe.

It is worth dwelling briefly on the alternative physical monist account of the world. Upon this theory, mental existence and the processes of human thought are wholly grounded in the physical world, which means that they are rendered the subject of scientific laws of either a deterministic or probabilistic kind. Free will is therefore a myth. The physics and chemistry in our heads determine the decisions that we make. The universe is closed. All that can happen is what is destined to happen. Leaving aside our own unenviable position in such a universe, it is evident that the circumstance of God the Creator is little better. At best he enjoys the excitement of a solitary dice thrower. At worst, he might as well settle for 'game over' and take the universe directly to its concluding state. Arguing a little more calmly, perhaps the best thing to say about physical monism is that it can form a reasonable accompaniment to atheism. As indicated, however, it does not seem to give a remotely satisfactory account of what we are as human beings or of our relationship with the physical world.

(In the preceding paragraph, God was referred to as 'he'. No gender implication was intended in so doing. In fact, there is nothing in the argument that would point in that direction. It is asked that, throughout this book, 'he' for the Creator should be understood as a contraction of 's/he'.)

Returning to the principal theme, the mental and physical dualism put forward in order to give a reasonable account of ourselves and the world in which we live also accommodates to the notion of a creation that is interesting and fulfilling to its divine Creator. But an acute problem remains. Does not the notion of wholly autonomous mental beings intrude upon the concept of God as omniscient and omnipotent? Yes, it does, but only in a similar manner to that raised by the schoolboy question: 'Can God make a stone so big that he cannot throw it away?' Whichever way one answers the schoolboy, there remains something that God cannot do! In similar fashion one can pose the question: 'Can God create a person with so much freedom that he cannot control or predict his actions?'

The problems and their solution come back to the Theory of Types, as identified in Chapter 3. Basically, if a view is taken of omnipotence and omniscience that ignores the Theory of Types and assumes that 'omni' should require no limit of any kind, then insoluble logical difficulties will ensue. Making a stone so big that you cannot throw it away must be a type of action one level above that of throwing it away, since the latter is contained within the notion of the stone being so big. Providing 'omni' is understood as applying to one type or the other, but not simultaneously to both, then choosing one answer or the other does not compromise omnipotence. Similar difficulties arise with freedom, and a similar solution is available.

It may be complained that this renders God subject to human logic, and that is something no one has any business to do. But is it human logic or just logic? Is logic something that we invent, in which case there may be some force in the complaint, or is it something that we discover, a facet of the existence that we experience. If it is the latter, then all that is being attempted is an explanation of the way things actually are in the relationship of God with human beings. That is the assumption upon which the argument will proceed.

Optimistic or Pessimistic

As indicated, the idea of God creating free human spirits who interact with the physical world need not compromise the related notions of his omnipotence and omniscience. But that is by no means the most daunting problem. Belief in God the Creator does not conclude with a declaration of his omnipotence. Holiness is equally an issue. Given the belief that God is the Creator, what happens if we try to use our knowledge of the natural world to work out something concerning his nature and purpose. What, for example, is to be made of the cry from Tennyson concerning the man of belief:

Who trusted God was love indeed
and love Creation's final law –
Tho' Nature red in tooth and claw
With ravine, shriek'd against his creed.[3]

Tennyson gives the problem vivid but only partial expression. To the moral problems of 'tooth and claw' must be added those of disease, famine, accident and ultimately mortality itself. We may believe that the world is a created world, but is it a good world created by a Holy God, or are there other more sinister elements to be taken into account? At this point, the argument bifurcates, with two quite different theistic routes available. They have been explored in depth by Jonathan Clatworthy, who describes them as belonging to theologies that are either 'optimistic' or 'pessimistic'.[4]

According to Clatworthy's penetrating account, an optimistic theology proceeds on the basis that a good God, with complete power and knowledge, created the world. A pessimistic theology agrees that there is an objective standard of goodness provided by a good God, but argues that the world does not measure up to that standard. There is an element of evil built into the way things are. Basically, the distinction between optimistic and pessimistic theologies is derived from different views of the presence of evil. For those following an optimistic theology, evil certainly exists, but it does so within a universe which is fundamentally good. It is permitted for the sake of good. There is no completely unredeemable evil. To pessimists this is too weak a response. Evil, far from being permitted by God, undermines God's control. The outcome, in practice although rarely in name, is a kind of polytheism. There is the one whom we call 'God', and then there are others, evil spirits perhaps, or the Devil, or some overriding principle of existence, by which God himself is constrained. These beings or principles exercise power independently of God and thus assume certain godlike capacities. Those who are on the side of God are in a continual state of conflict with the other (lesser) gods.

Although it outflanks some difficulties, the pessimistic route encounters fundamental obstacles. The notion of warring gods, with the human race caught somewhere in the middle, seems to have more to do with overwrought human imagination than anything actually to be found in the real world. As part of a natural theology, the metaphysics of creation, which are difficult enough anyway, become even more problematic in the face of rival powers. But a refusal to choose a pessimistic theology should not blind anyone to the force of the arguments that lead towards it. Tennyson's words about 'nature, red in tooth and claw' are more easily handled by a pessimistic theology than an optimistic one. Nor as indicated do the practical and moral problems of the natural order stop with those of predation. Accident, flood, famine and disease, all ravage the earth and bring untold misery upon humans and animals alike. Is God the omnipotent Creator responsible, and if so, what does this say about his moral state?

Within the boundaries of an optimistic theology, one possible way forward is to attribute such occurrences to a God-given autonomy of the natural order. After all, freedom has been a centrepiece of this whole argument, a necessary characteristic of life in the universe if it is to be interesting and satisfying to its Creator. But encouraging though such thoughts may seem to be, they do not appear to lead to a helpful answer. It is true that an individual spiritual being needs to be free, but the natural order itself does not seem to possess the characteristics of a being. A supposed autonomy of the natural order is not therefore to be compared with the autonomy of a human being. It is unclear what form such a grant of freedom could take and how it could operate. Perhaps there is a helpful answer that can be derived from this approach, but if so this text does not contain it.

An associated but seemingly neutral alternative is to regard natural events as originating independently of divine causation. In practice, this is a fairly common operational approach to accident, disaster and disease. But, in principle, it pushes the argument back toward a pessimistic theology. In effect, there are two Gods, one called 'God' and the other called 'Nature'. There is an understandable tendency not to look too hard at the principle, but it is still there!

The logical response, if an optimistic theology is still to be upheld, is to appeal to the idea of life in the hereafter. Whatever the shocks and chances of this world, opportunities will be available in the next life to recover from pain and suffering, and to rebuild relationships. (One can conjecture that the opportunities of the next world must be open to any creature capable of suffering, and not just to human beings. Only through such a conjecture does it seem logical to retain a belief in the moral perfection of God. Mere sentimentality? Why not mere morality?) Of course, the sceptical reply is that a life hereafter is merely being invented in a pathetic attempt to compensate for the obvious failures of the present life. In fact, nothing can be proved in either direction, but it does not follow that the sceptic must be allowed the last word. If the highest human aspiration points toward a God of moral perfection and a life beyond death, it is not an aspiration that is necessarily going to fail. Perhaps it is the opposite. Perhaps our highest aspirations on this earth reach only to the foothills of spiritual existence.

This argument helps to explain the tendency to combine belief in God the Creator with belief in an afterlife. The evil and suffering of the created world can only be redressed by a God of love and moral perfection through the opportunity of a further life. In large measure, therefore, the two beliefs are either held in concert, or they are doubted or abandoned in concert.

Focusing on the optimistic position, the notion that evil is permitted for the sake of a greater good needs very careful interpretation. Critically, it should not be claimed that things can ever become better as a result of evil. The pivotal point of the argument concerns the nature of freedom. Given the nature of individual human autonomy, that is to say the creation of beings with genuine free will, the point is not that God permits evil in order to generate a greater good, but rather that he cannot prevent evil if he is to provide the opportunity for good. A person must be free in order to love, to care, and to show compassion. But that same freedom may alternatively be used as the opportunity for evil. The distinction is subtle but crucial. The possibility of evil derives from the nature of freedom. It does not follow, however, that evil is an essential characteristic of existence. Evil deeds are rendered possible, they may be contingent upon existence, because individuals are free. But such deeds never make things better. The world would always be a better place if they were eschewed. Evil may be contingent, but it is never essential.

Optimism does not require therefore that it belongs within God's omnipotence to permit evil within certain limits in order to make things better in the long run. On the contrary, he can permit evil only in the sense that he cannot do otherwise if the universe is to be inhabited by autonomous spiritual beings. As previously argued, a universe without autonomous spiritual beings would be arid and without interest. Basically, it would seem that God does what he needs to do for the universe to be meaningful and satisfying to him and to those who live within it. This may seem to put a constraint upon God, but it is a constraint deriving only from the Theory of Types, which in logic cannot be avoided. Omnipotence does not mean the ability to perform the illogical!

Evil, then, is categorized as contingent upon existence, but not essential to it. That may be a significant piece of dialectic, but of course it does nothing to reduce the appalling consequences of actual sin upon individual human beings. However painful the subject, that is an issue to which the argument is frequently and unavoidably driven, reaching its conclusion in Chapter 7.

Communication

Accepting these points, the argument focuses once again upon the optimistic theme of an interesting universe inhabited by autonomous persons. Being autonomous means that individuals are free to think their own thoughts, make their own moral choices, and choose their own courses of action. How would or could the Creator of such an interesting universe relate to his creation?

At one extreme, it might be argued that having created a universe with independent spirits God would simply leave it alone to proceed in whatever way it collectively chose. Anything else would constitute divine interference and compromise the freedom of the individual. But such an answer would reduce the role of the Creator of the universe to that of observer in later times. In the context of previous remarks, it is difficult to imagine how mere observation, from everlasting to everlasting, would be sufficient to sustain interest, even harder to think that it could lead to ultimate fulfilment. So, if standing-off is not a sufficient answer, it follows that there must be some fuller relationship that God will be seeking with the subjects of his creation. A discussion of this relationship will continue in various parts of the forthcoming chapters. As a precursor, however, it will be helpful to look first at the problems involved in the actual establishing of communications.

Up to this point, the idea of relations between God and humankind has been explored without seriously questioning the means by which such relationships might come about. To begin the quest, how does a person meet his or her Creator? As a step toward an answer, how do human beings meet one another? The answer is through the operation of the senses. I am aware of myself as a spiritual being – or at least a conscious being – functioning within my own body. I use my senses to observe others whose actions are similar to mine, and assume that inside their bodies are conscious spiritual beings similar to myself. At least, that is how I intellectualize it, although actually the whole process is far more intuitive. It just seems to belong to human beings to know that other human beings exist, and that they can be communicated with, loved and cared for, or alternatively ignored or even hated. Solipsism, although it cannot be proved false, is not a serious option.

But while human beings are for the most part confident of the existence of others, in the sense of believing that others are aware and self-conscious, the medium of communication is almost entirely the physical world and the senses. Claims for direct mind-to-mind communication are sometimes made, but command no general or assured status. So the knowledge that one person has of another is gained by a combination of self-knowledge and the evidence of the senses.

In what ways then can a person become aware of and relate to his or her Creator? Clearly the intentions of the Creator for humankind can be thought about – if not actually known – through the interpretation of the everyday course of events or the discoveries of science. Alternatively, contact with God might be obtained through awareness of some public, supernatural or miraculous event. The dividing of the Red Sea to allow the passage of the Israelites, and the miraculous transformation by Jesus of water into wine, are examples, respectively, from the Old and New Testaments. But unlike communication via the physical world, is there also scope for direct contact, spiritual being to spiritual being, within the mental dimension$s$ as previously discussed? In fact, the Old Testament of the Bible is rich with claims for this kind of communication, whether it is a prophet proclaiming, 'Thus sayeth the Lord', or the boy Samuel, hearing the voice of the Lord in the night. (Although described as a voice, the biblical account makes it clear that it was a voice only able to be heard by the one person for whom it was intended.)

Given the reduction in formal religious beliefs, including beliefs based upon recorded revelation, problems associated with biblical claims for direct communication are bound to be substantial. Scepticism is liable to play a significant part, and even if scepticism is overcome, problems of interpretation will remain. But however serious those issues may be, probably of even greater importance is the problem of validating the source. Given the claim that a revelatory message has been received, how is the originator of that message to be identified? Often there seems to be an uncritical assumption that if a communication is received by other than ordinary physical means, then the recipient is bound to be clear about the origin. This phenomenon of uncritical assumption occurs with particular frequency in the Old Testament. To give just one example, in Exodus the Lord sets out for Moses the rules that the Israelites must observe for the treatment of slaves: benevolent rules, so that he who knocks out the eye of his slave girl must subsequently give the girl her freedom.[5] What is to be made of this? Slavery is wrong in principle, not just wrong in certain cruel implementations. But setting the rules legitimizes the process, and must therefore be an impossible activity for the Lord, unless we are prepared to contemplate the idea of God being morally inferior to at least some human beings. An alternative and for many people a more tenable explanation is that some ancient law-maker, anxious to codify slavery, was too easily persuaded that what he wanted to affirm had been put into his mind by the Almighty. This explanation overcomes the moral dilemma, but at the price of disclaiming the authenticity of the message.

How then is a message to be validated that has not arrived through any of the usual senses of the body. The answer is to refer to what constitutes the first characteristic of modern spirituality, the individual commitment to truth. As spiritual beings, independent members of an interesting universe, we must apply reason, conscience and 'heart' to the task of validating whatever information or message has been received, irrespective of whoever claims to have received it. We can seek the advice of others, and that may be of great value, but the accepting authority is still our own. No doubt reason, conscience and 'heart' can be imperfect instruments, but they are the only ones that we have been given. It behoves us therefore to use them as best we may, and not to accept uncritically the validity of whatever is claimed to have been received, or to make unconsidered assumptions about the sender. As a final point, this is not intended to discredit the idea of revelation. Caution is not the same as rejection! What needs to be recognized is that in the modern world claims of revelation are only likely to be accepted if they are made the subject of the most rigorous scrutiny.

Human beings also seek to communicate with God through their prayers – prayers that can be offered either in public or in private. As a subject, this is vast and profound. Given the emphasis upon secular spirituality, however, the function of prayer in the context of congregational worship will not be included in this discussion. Where private prayer is concerned, discussion will also be considerably limited due to the personal and subjective nature of the activity. What can be said is that among different people prayer does seem to encompass a great variety of behaviour and experience. For some people prayer is fundamental to their lives, for others in contrast it hardly even exists, and still others occupy a host of intermediate positions. What is important to remark is that in certain cases prayer followed by an exceptional sequence of events is regarded as providing a revelation – a revelation of the interpretive kind as it has been previously described. Where this occurs, however, the same criteria of validation will be needed as apply to other modes of revelation.

Here and Hereafter

Following these somewhat cautious remarks about revelation and prayer, what else needs to be said about the circumstances in which human beings can develop their relationship with God? According to the previous argument, for an existence to be interesting to its Creator individual spiritual beings need to be given autonomy, independence or freedom. This freedom must be of sufficient measure and duration to provide genuine choices of belief, conscience, decision and action. In such a life, individuals would then have the opportunity to enter freely into close relationships, both with their Creator and with one another. Intellectually this seems quite reasonable, but an immediate cautionary comment is required. Freedom in the social and political sphere must not be confused with anarchy, nor must freedom of action lapse into mere licence. How then should freedom be understood? The answer lies in the well-known expression: 'Freedom under the law.'

In order to enjoy a proper measure of freedom, the opportunities that it provides have to be exercised within the limits set by the law. This is a subject that will be given a detailed exploration in the next chapter. Anticipating one aspect of the outcome, what can be remarked at once is that the laws required are those that uphold human rights. Upon that basis, some further points can be made concerning the theology or metaphysic. According to the previous argument, an interesting universe is one in which the inhabitants are able to exercise a genuine freedom of belief, conscience, decision and action. In such a universe, individuals would have the opportunity to relate freely both to each other and to their Creator. But the exercise of freedom can only properly be undertaken within a framework of law that upholds human rights. It follows that these rights and laws would need to be identified with the Creator. Furthermore, it must be expected that the Creator would be prepared, at the last, to see that they are applied. It is in this context that the idea of eschatological change can be envisaged.

The mention of eschatological change ushers in the penultimate point. Hitherto the argument has focused primarily on life in the physical universe, the universe of space and time that we commonly experience. It is uncomfortably obvious, however, that the freedom upon which such emphasis has been placed has simply not been present for much of the history of the human race, and it remains unapplied to this day in many parts of the world. So the spiritual relations between the Creator of the universe and the creatures that live within it have often been constrained by the limitations of the social and political environment of the world. It could only be hoped therefore to bring them to fruition in the context of eternity. Within that vastly greater context, the Creator has to be recognized as the ultimate guarantor of the laws that underpin such freedoms. This notion can be given expression either through the concept of heaven, or of ultimate eschatological change in the state of the physical universe. But in either case the objective is the same, the positing of eternity as the context in which human rights and freedoms are upheld in order to provide the environment in which relationships with God and human beings can be brought to fruition.

It would be pleasing to conclude the argument at this point. Revelation and prayer constitute the means of communication between God and humankind. Caution is needed in accepting and interpreting revelation, but caution does not imply rejection. Freedom has emerged as a basic characteristic of secular spiritual life, joining the requirement for truth. Spiritual life is associated with beliefs in both a temporal and an eternal environment, granted by God the Creator so that spiritual relations can be fulfilled. In summary, that is where the discussion has reached. But stopping at that point would leave unfinished the earlier attempts to relate this approach to the Christian religious circumstances of our time. This issue is scheduled for consideration in later chapters, but it is still appropriate to add one immediate further comment. In an article entitled *Faith outside the Faiths*, Nicholas Henderson set out a liberal Christian perception of the contemporary attitudes and beliefs of people who were not in active membership of a Church or other religious body.[6] His conclusion, based in part upon the extraordinary national response to the death of the Princess of Wales, was that the public state of mind was definitely spiritual, even though it was not conventionally religious. In many ways this conclusion was encouraging, but it did also point toward a potential lack of spiritual stability. For many people, some form of religious belief will be needed if they are to maintain a coherent spiritual life. What needs to be asked is how far the beliefs in God and eternity explored in this chapter might be appropriate? Clearly they are more natural than biblical, but to persons reluctant to embrace formal doctrines that might not be a disadvantage. Probably what is most helpful about them is that they are also based upon the ideas of theological optimism. If the spiritual lives of those who entertain a 'faith outside the faiths' are to achieve a sense of coherence, it is a reasoned optimism that will be most appropriate to sustain them.

The Role of Doubt

Problems of doubt have been manifest throughout this chapter, and are destined to be present through much of the ensuing argument. In the context of belief in God, their influence raises a basic question. To summarize earlier points: we hope, fear, form opinions about and believe in far more than we can ever know. We do so because the world we live in drives us in that direction. The question is why? Why has God put us into a world with so little knowledge and so many uncertainties? Within the framework of theistic belief there are two quite different answers, associated respectively with optimistic and pessimistic theologies.

Taking the pessimistic argument first and expressing it in extreme form, in a mysterious world it is assumed that God will give sufficient guidance to those that he has chosen to enable them to believe what is true and thus find salvation. The remainder are justly condemned. Underlying this approach is the thought that, in the absence of mystery and doubt, right belief would be open to all simply by the exercise of the intellect. As some evil beings are destined to suffer the wrath of God, not his redemption, the world requires the element of mystery in order that salvation can be made wholly dependent upon faith. That is to express the pessimistic approach in its harshest form – a form that it must be hoped would attract little support today, although it was certainly implicit in some of the earlier formulations of Christian doctrine.

The alternative optimistic approach could hardly be more different. In the absence of certainty, it is argued that it behoves us to accept the right of others to hold different beliefs, and to provide support for others in their doubts and unbeliefs. God has created humankind in such a way that individual spiritual development becomes the stronger for respecting the different beliefs, doubts and unbeliefs of others, and upholding their right to own them. To this end, limited knowledge, different beliefs and unavoidable doubts characterize the world into which we have been created. Our shared humanity includes a sharing of ignorance. Learning to live together in ignorance and doubt is part of what it is to be human, and only as we become fully human can we enter into the right relationship with the God who is our Creator.

To an extent, the optimistic approach constitutes a way forward rather than an explanation, but perhaps that is the most that can hoped for in this present life. Question marks can of course be put against both the optimistic and pessimistic accounts. Some may want to turn away from theistic belief altogether. As the optimistic approach was preferred in the earlier discussion, however, and is consistently more appropriate for the development of a secular spirituality, it will be sustained here and broadly applied in later chapters. On a positive basis, doubt will be treated not as something that one should strive continuously to overcome but as an unavoidable component of human life on earth.

God and Being

This section is almost an appendix to this chapter. Virtually everything that has been argued about God the Creator – and for that matter virtually everything that most Churches say about God – fits with the general notion that God is a being, or more reverently a Being. Upon that understanding, God is the supreme mind, regarded as either omnipotent and omniscient or at least more powerful and knowledgeable than anyone else. He is also supremely good and wise. It was upon assumptions like these that the questions of optimism and pessimism have been pursued, and thoughts set out concerning an interesting universe. But there are difficulties implicit in these assumptions, difficulties that have led some theologians to develop alternative ideas. Here are some of the thoughts.

If God is a being, or more reverently a Being, then he is one spiritual being among other spiritual beings, albeit the Supreme Being. For some people, this is not a comfortable position. Dorothy Emmett, for example, does not want to regard God as a member of a class, even a class with only one member. What she expresses is the concern that it seems conceptually inadequate and perhaps irreverent to attempt to contain God within our human classifications.[7] Upon that thought, God is not the solitary member of the class of divine beings. The term 'solitary' would rescue us from polytheism, but the thought remains that God creates and sustains all that exists, and is not just a part of it.

Likewise, God is the source of all that we can classify, not a member of a class.

The difficulty on the other side is that virtually all the terms that people use in talking about God – speaking of him as King, Judge, Lord of Hosts, and claiming that he acts in certain ways – point in the direction of God as a Being, even if always the Supreme Being, and this takes us back in the direction of merely human classification.

Perhaps this is an unavoidable consequence of human autonomy. If God creates free spiritual beings with the capacity to form mental concepts both of the world around them and of their creator, perhaps it is inevitable that they will think in ways that include their creator within their classifications. Whisper it softly, but perhaps it is even more than that. Perhaps the creation of free spirits is a kind of self-denying ordinance, so that God becomes one being, albeit the Supreme Being, in a universe of many beings. Perhaps this is yet another consequence of the Theory of Types. Then again, perhaps this is nonsense or worse! Perhaps it would be wise to walk away quickly from such reckless conceptions.

What is to be done about it? One possibility, the one normally used in this text, is to continue to address God and think about him as if he were a being, but endeavour always to recognize and acknowledge that such ways of thinking are conceptually inadequate. Care is needed with such a course of action, because an inadequate expression can on occasions mislead, or even be worse than no expression at all. One alternative would be to refuse to say anything whatsoever about God. Whereof one cannot speak, one had best keep silent! This is a possibility with a kind of attraction. A book about spiritual life which included nothing about God might achieve a certain notoriety! As a continuation of the present approach, however, this would omit far too much that is significant for it to be considered as a serious option.

Another possibility, a possibility brought to widespread attention in this country in the 1960s with the publishing of *Honest to God* by John Robinson, is to recast altogether the way of thinking about God. This is exemplified by saying that God is not *a* being at all but either Being itself, or if not being itself then the ultimate depth of Being. According to Robinson, 'The word "God" denotes the ultimate depth of all our being, the creative ground and meaning of all our existence.'[8] A similar thought is adopted by Chris Scott, who writes: 'We then talk about God not as a being, but simply as Being.'[9] Finally, John Macquarrie extends this way of thinking by arguing that 'God' is the religious word that is applicable to Being when Being is believed to be gracious. It follows that the words 'God' and 'Being' are not synonyms, as Being would not be called 'God' if Being were believed to be indifferent or cruel.[11] Other variations upon this theme have used the word 'God' to denote ultimate concern or ultimate reality. What characterizes them all is the wish to depart from the idea that God is the supreme mind or the supreme being, or perhaps even the Supreme Being.

As indicated, there are difficulties with these ideas. Firstly, there is the problem of why the term 'being' is rendered 'Being'. When it comes to individual beings, it is quite reasonable to agree that the presence of the most significant amongst them should be identified and dignified with a capital letter. There is or can be a properly explained difference between 'a being' and 'a Being', the latter being applied particularly to indicate a divine presence. But is there any corresponding argument to explain why the term 'being' should be replaced by 'Being', when the term is used without an article? Presumably, the intention is to indicate the belief that existence itself is divine or gracious. The danger with such a usage of capitals is that it can all too easily lead to confusion or misunderstanding. Where possible, this text will manage without the capitals.

Secondly, it is not clear that being requires or possesses either a ground or a depth. Certainly existence or being is a mystery, but it is doubtful if we make any progress with the mystery by transferring it to a ground or depth! Of course, by ground of being one might mean the creator of all that exists, but this would simply return the argument to the idea of God the Creator, the Supreme Being. As the intention was to avoid such a way of thinking, that particular interpretation would be self-defeating.

The most serious problem, however, is that actions cannot ordinarily be ascribed to Being itself, or to ultimate concern or ultimate reality, but only to individual existent beings. To illustrate the point, suppose that Tom helps Harry change a wheel on his car. It might be claimed that Tom behaves in this way because of his kindly disposition, because it belongs to the nature of his being to act in such a manner. But it would still be Tom who helps to change the wheel, not Tom's disposition or the nature of Tom's being. So it is with all activities. Beings carry out activities, not being itself or the depth of being or the ground of being!

Where does this leave statements of the kind 'God creates . . .', or 'God loves . . .', or 'God responds . . .'? None of them seem to be applicable if God is to be regarded as being itself or ultimate reality or any other 'not a being', if it can be put like that. A possible way forward is to argue that that God-talk is different from everyday-talk, and that language may be applied in a special way when speaking of God. But such an approach has to be treated with great care. God-talk may extend (will often extend) beyond everyday-talk, but should not be disconnected from it or contradict it lest words become merely confusing and lose significance.

The problem is that there are times when believers do want to think of God in an active sense – creating, loving, forgiving – and are obliged therefore by the limitations of understanding to think of him as the Supreme Being, the being who engages in these activities. These thoughts can be qualified by asserting that in ways beyond human comprehension God is above and beyond the idea of a Supreme Being, that he is the source of all that exists and is not limited by being a part of it. Of course, the latter assertion may be too vague to be of much substance, but at least it is an attempt to recognize that the human ability to think about God is fundamentally limited. Proceeding in that way does at least provide some rationale for the earlier metaphysical explorations.

But what of the notion that God is being itself, not a being. Bluntly, it seems that if a person wishes to hold to that notion, or to any of the associated ideas, then he or she will have to eschew nearly all active verbs when talking of God. That may not be a good reason for departing from such ideas, but holding to it is likely to be a hard discipline.

Let us finish by applying these thoughts in the only way that seems to connect with the previous arguments. Looking at the spiritual lives of human beings, if God is being, which means that existence is gracious, then belief in God is the belief that it belongs to the nature of existence for loving relations to endure and find ultimate fulfilment. It is manifestly in the nature of being that reconciliation and loving relationships are possible – indeed they are frequent occurrences in many lives. The question is whether they are ultimately triumphant? Clearly, for being to be gracious, for love to endure the shocks and chances of this life and to triumph over death itself, there is a requirement that life itself continues beyond death. Moreover it must be life of such a kind that love can be fulfilled. That is the vital point. Being is not gracious if the end of a loving relationship is the sad retreat from the graveside. So according to this manner of thinking, belief in God is not belief in a Supreme Being who loves, forgives and resurrects, but belief that the nature of being itself is such that reconciliation and loving relationships ultimately overcome the worst vicissitudes of this or any other life (or death). It contrasts, for example, with the grim conviction of Thomas Hardy that nature and being are indifferent to human suffering, and that time is cruel and insatiable. Upon that understanding, it is at least possible to empathize with these different ideas, although they still remain separate from the central theme.

Notes

1. Cecil Frances Alexander, *There is a green hill far away*, 1848.
2. Occam's Razor. Principle of economy named after William of Occam, c. 1300, who argued that explanations should never be needlessly complicated.
3. Alfred Lord Tennyson, *In Memoriam*, 1850. Written to commemorate the death of a friend, it formed an elegy on a Victorian faith that was gradually weakening.
4. Jonathan Clatworthy, *Good God,* Jon Carpenter Publishing, 1997.
5. Exodus 21:26–7.
6. Revd Nicholas Henderson, 'Faith Outside the Faiths: A Continuing Dilemma', in the MCU Book of Essays, The New Liberalism, 1998.
7. Dorothy Emmett, 'Could God be a Person', *Modern Believing*, Modern

Churchpeople's Union Journal, vol. XXXVII, no. 1, 1996, p. 7.
8. John A. T. Robinson, *Honest to God*, SCM, 1963, p. 47.
9. Chris S. Scott, *Between the Poles*, New Millennium, 1996, p. 65.
10. John Macquarrie, '*How is Theology Possible*', in *The Honest to God Debate*, SCM, 1963.

5
Freedom and Human Rights

Characteristics of Freedom

In Chapter 4 it was suggested that a universe would only become interesting and satisfying to its Creator if individual spiritual beings with autonomy, independence and freedom were living within it. Accurate or not, that conjecture was certainly not necessary as a precursor to an exploration of freedom and human rights. On the contrary, the issue of freedom often becomes prominent in human affairs in ways that are independent of any religious consideration. Furthermore, the choice of a somewhat elliptical approach to freedom left a number of important problems and subtleties untouched. What follows, therefore, is an exploration of freedom on a much broader basis, with the religious element only entering the discussion at a later stage.

The first point to note is that freedom exists in two different though often closely related modes. The two modes can be distinguished as *'freedom from'* and *'freedom to'*. The former, which is the more elementary, is simply freedom identified negatively as the absence of constraint. The second is freedom in the more developed sense of opportunity, including particularly the opportunity to hold beliefs, to attempt tasks or acquire possessions. Metaphorically speaking, *'freedom from'* and *'freedom to'* are two sides of the same coin, but confusion can arise if the distinction between them is inadequately recognized.

An important characteristic of freedom is that it is almost never absolute. To demonstrate this characteristic, a simple, if fairly lurid, example is utilized. Consider freedom in the form of the opportunity to do either A or B where:

A = Stay sensibly away from the edge of the cliff.
B = Jump off the edge of the cliff.
Note that the theoretical opportunity C does not actually exist:
C = Step off the cliff edge, hover for thirty seconds, then return to the surface.

Perhaps, in another world, with a different more ethereal body, C might become a genuine opportunity, but in the real physical world a person can only choose between A and B. Option C is simply not available. Nor would it be difficult to think of other notional options that would be similarly absent. Simple and primitive though this example is, it does demonstrate one inescapable characteristic of freedom, when viewed in the sense of opportunity. It can never be absolute! Only some opportunities will be present. Others that can be theoretically described will in practice be absent.

What of freedom in the more elementary sense of freedom from constraint? It might be claimed that a single particle in an otherwise empty space is absolutely free. That is true in the formal sense, but it is also true that there is absolutely nothing that the particle can do! If freedom is just the absence of constraint, then it could at least notionally be absolute, but such a concept of freedom is itself very limited, and as soon as the idea extends to opportunity then the freedom available is invariably limited in its scope. For human beings, it transpires that the forms these various limitations can take are fourfold.

In the first place, there are direct constraints or limitations, one rather fanciful example of which has been given above. In fact, the constraints are many, and include the temporal nature of life. None of us chooses where or when to be born. It happens as it does, and thus presents us with some opportunities and denies us others. Nor is it just physical constraints that are imposed upon our lives. Whilst we possess mental capabilities we also have mental limitations, so that we have the opportunity to think some thoughts but not others, and to make some decisions but not others. Whether physical or mental, these are all direct constraints.

Next, there exist what may be described as consequential constraints. For example, suppose James can choose between two courses of action, A or B, but, if he chooses B, he will receive a lethal electric shock. Whilst this is only an indirect constraint, it is also a very potent one!

Thirdly, there are moral constraints. James can choose between courses of action A and B, but he believes that B is morally wrong. Once again, this is an indirect constraint.

Finally, there is a form of constraint upon freedom that arises from the problems of type that were discussed in Chapter 3. If type had previously seemed abstract and theoretical, here it becomes real and serious indeed. Let us proceed by example. Suppose Tom allows Dick the freedom to lock up Harry. Then clearly Harry's freedom has been denied. But if Tom constrains Dick, so that he cannot lock up Harry, then Dick's freedom has been limited. Of course, the freedom of Dick to lock up Harry is a different type or level of freedom from the freedom of Harry that is lost by his being locked up, but that is not a point likely to provide much comfort to Harry!

Freedom then has some strange characteristics. Without the freedom to make decisions, human beings would simply not exist in the way that we understand them. So freedom, in the sense of the capacity to exercise free will, is an absolute necessity for human existence, yet freedom itself is hardly ever absolute. Free will means that we have the opportunity to think some thoughts, but not others, and to take and implement some decisions, but not others. Freedom is at the same time both essential and limited.

Given this strange start, it is unsurprising that the problems associated with freedom continue to grow as consideration moves from one person to many, and from the internal exercise of personal free will to the external exercise of social opportunity. If Harry is stranded alone on a desert island, he is not in any danger of being locked up by Dick, but in the absence of Tom, Dick and other members of the human race, his choice of action is going to be severely limited. Society brings with it constraints upon freedom in the form of moral issues and sometimes the problems of type as previously discussed, but it also brings a host of opportunities that would simply not be available to one individual alone. In any case, life in society is not a matter of choice for most of us. We are born into it, and must make our way within it as best we can.

If human life is to be lived within society, how are the problems of freedom to be addressed? In particular, using an earlier example, what can be done to help Harry confront the problem of being locked up by Dick? The answer, general enough to be of value even when connected to this somewhat starkly presented problem, is embodied in the well-known principle of freedom under the law.

According to the law, Dick can only lock up Harry for due cause. Thus both Dick and Harry enjoy their proper measure of freedom, exercised within the limits set by the law.

The Origin and Nature of Human Rights

Inevitably the idea of 'freedom under the law' raises further questions, of which the first two are as follows. To whom belongs the law, and of what is it composed?

With regard to ownership, in most cases the laws themselves are those that have been established by the nation state. In a generic sense, therefore, they are tribal in origin. Tribalism, in one or other manifestation, is common to much of life, and contributes powerfully to the framework of our lives. Where freedom is concerned, it is the tribe or nation that provides freedom (in both senses) and protects it, and it is also the tribe or nation that from time to time constrains it. Patriotic songs give emotional expression to the protective role. Sadly and even tragically, if the tribe or nation falls into the wrong hands, it can become the vehicle of savage oppression and thereby the means of denying even the most elementary of freedoms. In that respect, one need think no further than the slave-based societies that were prolific in the past.

The laws provided by the tribe or state are not confined to issues of freedom. Among others, they also govern matters such as education, health and safety, care of the elderly, transport, business, and of course taxation! In general, they provide citizens with their civic rights. Freedom, in its various manifestations, is nested within this much broader grouping. Civic rights include the right to individual freedom, the right to enjoy opportunity, but freedom must vie with other rights that may be regarded as equally desirable or sometimes even preferable.

At some point in human history, the idea of civic rights conferred by the nation state extended to the idea of human rights – rights belonging to an individual human being simply because he or she was human. This development was of fundamental importance in human affairs. Although this is not an historical text, some brief comments will be offered nevertheless concerning the manner in which this development came about.

As a preliminary point, there is a tendency to think that the progress of ideas depends principally upon the work of a few intellectual giants. In religious and scientific spheres this may and often will be the case, but in contrast the concepts that led to human rights owe much more to the common perceptions of ordinary people. To give an important if somewhat oblique example, the origin of Anglo-Saxon liberal democracy as practised in the United Kingdom and the United States is often traced to the political philosophy of John Locke. It is not difficult to demonstrate the association, but it remains questionable how far the limitations of John Locke's thought to the advance of the *bourgeois* should be regarded as imposing constraints upon the democratic structures of the two nations. Judging from the way that they separately developed, it would seem that the strengths and weaknesses of democracy in Britain and America should be associated chiefly with the collective characteristics of their peoples, not the political philosophy of one person no matter how distinguished. In like manner, any general thrust towards human rights has to be seen chiefly as a movement of people, an idea that must take root in whole communities if it is to be effective. No doubt particular individuals have an important part to play, but neither praise nor blame should attach too greatly to any one person.

A commonly expressed view of human rights is that they have a specifically Christian origin. A positive and detailed account of this view is given by Larry Siedentop in his book, *Democracy in Europe*.[1] Given the immense influence of Christianity upon the western world, a relationship between the social influence of the religion and the espousal of human rights is clearly to be expected. The question, however, is whether that relationship is one of causation. In particular, what needs to be determined is how far the liberal modes of thought that lead to human rights have a Christian origin. The issue is problematic. Christianity has many strands, only some of which have a distinctly liberal character. Others are fundamentalist in nature, and far removed from liberal ideas. In consequence, it is doubtful how far it is valid to regard Christianity itself as an antecedent of liberalism and of human rights. In this connection, the argument put forward by Paul Badham in his study of Modernist theology is of particular significance. Badham sees the rise of an autonomous ethic as a major factor in the Victorian crisis of faith, as people who felt that they had discovered a higher ethic challenged the traditional morality of an earlier Christianity.[2] Given the validity of this argument, it is not difficult to conceive a rising commitment to human rights occurring in association with the development of the autonomous ethic. The two would emerge as natural partners, obtaining succour one from another.

It seems reasonable therefore to assume that the emergence of human rights out of nationally based civic rights was primarily an autonomous secular development. Using that assumption, it becomes possible to sketch quite briefly the principal steps in the progression of freedom and human rights to their climax in the adoption by the United Nations of the Universal Declaration of Human Rights.[3]

In this country, the first hint of civic rights goes back to the beginnings of English common law at the time of Alfred the Great. A subsequent limited but crucial step was taken in 1215 when King John was persuaded by his barons to sign Magna Carta at Runnymede. Scholars have pored over the clauses themselves and they are of great interest, but what was more important was the actual process of signing. By the very act of signing the document (attaching his seal), the King bound himself by the same laws that applied to his subjects. Henceforward, no one was above the law.

At the time, of course, the rights contained in Magna Carta were applicable only to the relatively small number of persons who were freemen, but gradually, with the departure of the feudal system, they came to embrace more and more of the populace. But they were still rights confined to the people of just one nation, and it would be many years before the idea of universal human rights would take root. Indeed, even as the notion of freedom and the rights of citizens was gaining ground in Europe, so colonial expansion and the use of slaves in America were busily denying those concepts overseas. The scene in North America was one of notable inconsistency, with the leaders of the American Revolution drawing up the statement in 1776 declaring: 'We hold these truths to be self-evident, that all men are created equal, that they are endowed by their Creator with certain unalienable rights; that amongst these are life, liberty and the pursuit of happiness . . .'[4] Unfortunately, the reference to 'all men' failed at the time to secure the rights of either indigenous Americans or African slaves.

Back in Europe, the French Revolution led to the Declaration of the Rights of Man and of Citizens by the French National Assembly in 1789, but in the immediate aftermath events in France failed to uphold the principles that it proclaimed. Moving forward to the nineteenth century, John Stuart Mill could write persuasively of the virtues of freedom, but still deny it to the peoples of the empire on the grounds that they were yet as children and remained in need of external control.[5] Some semblance of that attitude persisted right up to the 1930s, so that children of that era could enjoy reading *Sanders of the River* and cheerfully embrace the concept of the paternalistic white man and his empire. It seems strange now to look back, and realize just how very recent is the common perception of freedom as the birth right of every human being.

But the object of this survey is to chart the growth of the new thinking, not to point accusing fingers at the old. Without needing to argue that morality is entirely relative, one can recognize that it is not wholly unchanging and understand that it is all too easy to make critical judgements of yesterday's behaviour by applying today's standards. Returning briefly to the historical theme, the historian John Elliott offered the thesis that the discovery of the New World brought with it new challenges to religious and philosophical thinking, challenges that made an important contribution to the emergence of the concepts of human commonalty and human rights.[6] This contributes to the more general argument that the gradual widening of human experience, whether through exploration, scientific advance, or other form of educational study, has played a vital part in the growth of the new and comprehensive approach to humankind.

To come up to date, at the conclusion of a patchwork of developments spanning many centuries, the concept of human rights finally achieved broadly based recognition when the Universal Declaration of Human Rights was adopted and proclaimed by the General Assembly of the United Nations on 10 December 1948. Notwithstanding the long road to its achievement, the Universal Declaration was very much a creature of its time, written in the immediate aftermath of World War Two, when the world was still recoiling in horror at the discovery of the full extent of the Jewish Holocaust and other Nazi persecutions. It was also written in that brief interlude before the Cold War clamped itself fully upon the post-war world. As such the Universal Declaration had a tendency to be both reactive and over-enthusiastic. Whilst it spelt out in necessary detail those rights and freedoms that should prevent a resurgence of mass killings, it also attempted to introduce forms of social engineering that would later seem appropriate neither to the times of the Cold War nor its market-orientated successor.

Whatever its weaknesses, however, the Universal Declaration marked a sea change in human thought and aspiration. It had taken a long time to advance from the recognition of civic freedom, but gradually from national endeavour and patriotic sentiment there had emerged the appreciation that all human beings should be free by common right, and not only as a privilege of national citizenship. In similar fashion, the sense of freedom for all human beings by right had proceeded slowly to the more broadly based concept of human rights. That long process reached its climax in December 1948 when the General Assembly of the

United Nations solemnly adopted the Universal Declaration of Human Rights. That, in a word, is the point to which freedom has at last taken us.

The response to the Universal Declaration over the last fifty years has varied greatly from one place and situation to another. At the time of its adoption, there seemed to be an acute reluctance by governments to publicize what they had done. In some parts of the world, the most terrible atrocities continued to be practised, in blatant defiance of everything that the Declaration stood for. More encouragingly, following the growth of human rights organizations such as Amnesty International and Human Rights Watch, much more serious efforts have been made by the international community to halt such actions and to bring their perpetrators to justice. At the beginning of the new millennium, freedom and human rights have become a part of the political and social agenda in a manner that has never previously obtained. Clearly, there is much more that could be written on this subject, and some particular points will be made later in Chapter 8.

At this stage, however, it is the rights themselves upon which the focus will be maintained, the rights and their relationship with freedom, and the grounds (or otherwise) for their inclusion in the Universal Declaration. As has been remarked, the advance from the freedom of members of a tribe (nation) to the rights of members of the human race involved two distinct steps. One was the step from tribal to universal application, a step that has been charted here only to a very limited extent and about which some historical question marks remain. The second is the step from a set of freedoms to a set of human rights. What are or should be included in the latter? That is the question now to be addressed.

Given the fundamental importance of freedom, the right to 'life, liberty and security of person' will be dominant in almost any list of human rights, and will clearly need to be supported by an appropriate set of ancillary rights. But how far should the rights extend beyond that? There is a persistent tendency to expand the list, and the wisdom of that process is certainly open to question. It is one thing to insist that people should be free to help one another, another to insist that they should be obliged to help one another, that it is a human right to be helped! The temptation to seek a progressive extension of the right to be helped is one that enthusiasts for human rights find it very difficult to resist. In so doing, they not only render human rights more numerous, more controversial and more difficult to defend, they also ultimately risk compromising some of those very rights to freedom around which the whole process began. To put it in fairly sharp terms, there is a temptation to use human rights as a vehicle for social engineering, to use them in pursuit of a particular kind of society, instead of using them to liberate people, so that they can determine their own kind of society.

There is a strong case for arguing that human rights should be few in number, and that those few should be most rigorously upheld. Given the right to 'life, liberty and security of person', the essential supporting rights are those that provide freedom from slavery, arbitrary detention and torture, that secure a basic standard of living and give the equal protection of the law to every individual. Rights to freedom of thought, conscience and religion, and their peaceful expression, are also vital. Beyond that, however, the tendency is to move from what is essential to what is desirable, from what could and should be made straightforwardly available to every human being, to what persons with active social consciences believe would be desirable for every human being. It is not a question of being cynical about the additions. In many cases persons of good will would actively support them as desirable features of a charitable and responsible society, but that is not in itself sufficient cause to promote them as human rights.

Let us examine some examples. The Universal Declaration of Human Rights asserts that everyone has the right to education. That is fine. Deliberately to deprive a child (or anyone else) of education is an abuse. But the declaration goes on to insist that compulsory elementary education should be free for every child. Now the commitment to education is widespread, and many people would happily support the provision of free elementary education as a desirable feature for any reasonably affluent and organized society. But what of a poverty-stricken and disorganized society? There is no such thing as a free lesson, any more than there is a free lunch! Someone has to pay. By 'free' is presumably meant 'free at the point of delivery'. So an impoverished government, struggling perhaps with famine and a desperate need to provide clean water, is guilty of human rights abuses if it is unable in some cases to provide free education, or if it decides that free education is not at the top of its priority list. That is not a sustainable position. Education is a right, but the mode of delivery should be at the discretion of individual societies. Furthermore, there is a distinction to be drawn between those rights that could apply to any society at any time, like not torturing people, and those that require substantial levels of material wealth and organization, like free elementary education, in order to be provided. The first are human rights, or should be, the second are desirable characteristics of a developed society, or may be.

The second example is sharper. The Universal Declaration demands equal pay for equal work. As a principle, it seems fine, but look a little closer. First, as it is a human right, it should be globally applicable. In practice, that would be virtually impossible without a quite staggering level of communication and organization. Secondly, there is no indication in the Universal Declaration as to who should determine the level of this 'equal' pay. In the wrong hands, it could easily turn the right to 'equal' pay into the 'right' to equal poverty! But the third point is the most critical. The determination of equal pay by some third party is a denial of the right of the individual freely to negotiate his own contract of employment. In a market-orientated society, the freedom to negotiate occupies a position of fundamental importance, and in that regard the posited right to equal pay in the Universal Declaration takes away far more than it confers. In conclusion, it appears that human rights, as they have been internationally negotiated, have not only been too expansive but have also included some quite inappropriate clauses.

The last comment obviously chimes with the view that human rights should be confined chiefly to those essential to guarantee life and individual freedom. It should perhaps be added that there would be no shortage of persons who would disagree. From a social reforming standpoint, it can be argued that the articles of the Universal Declaration, as well as providing protection for individuals against the kind of horrors so recently perpetrated in the Jewish Holocaust and elsewhere, could usefully be applied to foster some desirable elements of social engineering. But the approach to human rights advocated herein is related more narrowly to individual freedom, and is therefore concerned mainly with rights necessary for a person to form his or her own beliefs and to act (peacefully) upon them. As previously indicated, the Universal Declaration moves some distance beyond that minimum requirement.

Briefly to explore the Universal Declaration itself, article 3, stating that everyone has the right to life, liberty and security of person, establishes the basis of the declaration. In immediate support are the articles requiring that no one shall be held in slavery, subjected to arbitrary arrest or tortured. Also of fundamental importance to individual liberty are articles affirming the right of recognition before the law, and the right to freedom of thought, conscience and religion. Other articles uphold the right to marry, to found a family, and to own property. Given the previously expressed preference for a limited set of rights, questions arise with regard to the last three. One approach would be to follow English common law, which presumes that a person is free to do anything that the law does not explicitly forbid. With freedom understood in that way, the need for detail in expressing a number of human rights would be obviated. As the thinking underlying English common law is not universally accepted, however, it may be desirable to spell out at least some of the details of individual freedom. Late in the list, but nevertheless essential, is the article declaring the right to an adequate standard of living. Unsurprisingly, given the origin of the Universal Declaration, the right to nationality is proclaimed, and then come the articles that set out the manner in which individual nations should arrange matters for their inhabitants. Suffice it to remark that these clauses, being organizational in content, are very different from those that proclaim the essential safeguards for life and individual freedom. The Universal Declaration is arguably the most important and valuable document of the twentieth century, but it is not without its imperfections.

There are two further points that are worth noting. The first is that the Universal Declaration does not of itself constitute a statement of law. Rather it establishes a set of principles upon which international and national law should be based. The second concerns the question of how to combine the different rights and freedoms. Amnesty International asserts that the rights are indivisible, but it is difficult to support that position in logic, and it can only reasonably be regarded as a kind of distant aspiration. In reality, any reasonably civilized country would find great difficulty in framing laws that simultaneously sustained all the rights and freedoms contained in the Universal Declaration. Criminal law and judicial processes, for example, will struggle to find the right balance between the rights of alleged criminals and the protection of victims. In some cases, the rights of one individual may appear to be in outright opposition to the rights of another. As indicated, one solution would be to establish a slimmer set of rights and then make a more determined effort nationally and internationally to uphold them. What is certainly needed is a new debate. Human rights groups tend at present to be somewhat uncritical in their approach to the Universal Declaration. As a result they are reluctant to engage in any very meaningful discussion about its content with political parties or governmental authorities. There is still much that needs to be done!

Tribalism in Politics and Religion

Historically, human rights have developed out of national politics and reached the international stage through the involvement and associated development of the United Nations. Socially and attitudinally, they have struggled to emerge from a global society in which tribalism seems always to have had a dominant role. The term 'tribal' is applied in a generic sense. It may take the form of nationalism, it may be commitment to regiment, club, firm or union, it may be tribalism in the precise sense of the word, but whatever its particular manifestation, it is almost always present and occupying a significant and often dominant place in human life.

Part of the essence of tribalism is that it excludes. Those who are not part of the tribe – whatever the tribe may be – are treated differently and often less favourably than those who are. It is therefore liable to be antipathetic to human rights. It does not have to be. It is not beyond human wit and wisdom to be tribally active and yet recognize that there are some behavioural characteristics that are beyond tribalism and must be extended to the entirety of the human race. Tragically, in the political sphere, that has often not been the case, with extremities of left and right wing political beliefs being particularly deadly in their approach to human rights. Organized religion likewise has a somewhat chequered history where the development of human rights is concerned, as will now be discussed.

On a narrowly rational basis, it might be expected that theistic religion, in relating human beings to the one Creator of all things and all men, would be above and beyond tribalism in any of its manifestations. But narrow rationalism would be badly wrong! Sadly and tragically, the great theistic religions of Judaism and Christianity have both become intertwined with the human tribal scene. (Comment in this text is not being extended to other theistic religions.)

Certain Old Testament passages are tribal in the narrow sense. In Genesis the words of the Lord to Abraham are given as follows:

> I make this covenant, and I make it with you: you shall be the father of a host of nations. .... I will fulfil my covenant between myself and you and your descendants after you, generation after generation, an everlasting covenant, to be your God, yours and your descendants after you. As an everlasting possession I will give you and your descendants after you the land in which you now are aliens, all the land of Canaan, and I will be God to your descendants.[7]

According to this text, the one eternal God covenants with one small part of the human race, and does so in a way that virtually guarantees that the land of Canaan will run with blood. Whilst other Old Testament texts provide a very different message, the availability of texts such as this one provides a direct religious encouragement for actions that are wholly inimical to human rights.

With the New Testament, commitments to narrow tribalism depart, but are replaced by a new tribalism of faith. Christianity, in its more exclusive modes, identifies the elect of God, those whom he has chosen, and who demonstrate their election by their faith.

The roots of this tribalism of faith are found in unexpected passages of the New Testament. For example, the Gospel according to St John contains the assertion: 'For God so loved the world that he gave his only begotten Son, that whosoever believeth in him should not perish, but have everlasting life.'[8] These words, inspirational for so many, contain a danger. The problem is the 'whosoever believeth in him'. Christians of an exclusivist, fundamentalist persuasion recognize four categories of believers and unbelievers: the true believers (the elect of God), heretics, Jews and the heathen.

According to the exclusivist belief, only the elect of God will enjoy everlasting life. The remainder are destined to perish or worse. This sense of the divisions of man is strengthened by New Testament prophecies. In the Gospel according to St Matthew is written: 'So shall also the coming of the Son of Man be. Then shall two be in the field; the one shall be taken and the other left. Two women shall be grinding at the mill; the one shall be taken, and the other left.'[9] In this text, there is no sense at all of the Son of Man acting for the whole of humanity. The divisions wrought by God are more fundamental than the common bonds of humankind.

Clearly the use of biblical texts in the above argument is highly selective, and other choices would point in quite different directions. The problem is that when tribal attitudes are to the fore, these are just the kind of texts that are going to be used. For many centuries, the consequences of this tribalism in religious faith were appalling. In Europe, witches and heretics were burned to death, and torture became institutionalized in the Inquisition. In the Americas and in Africa, colonial expansion led to vast numbers of those who were categorized as heathen being slaughtered or enslaved. In so remarking, it is also important to recognize that human wickedness arises in many different ways, and that religion frequently opposes it and seeks to mitigate its consequences. But it does seem that if tribalism becomes a dominant characteristic in a religion, then that religion will also acquire an alarming capacity to ignore even the most elementary rights of those who are excluded from its fold.

With regard to Christendom, the extraordinary thing is that Jesus taught his followers to love God and to love their neighbours, and this message has been solemnly handed down from one generation of Christians to another for nearly two thousand years. Yet it seems that once tribalism, in whatever form, becomes engaged in a religion, then an injunction to behave well toward others becomes interpreted as being applicable only to persons within the tribe. Outside the tribe, there seem to be no religious barriers to prevent the most atrocious behaviour. Worst of all are those cases where religious belief, far from discouraging atrocities, actually provides the justification for implementing them. If torturing a heretic will persuade him to recant from his wrong beliefs, and thus enable him to have his soul saved, then torturing him becomes a good thing to do. And even if he refuses to recant, the example of his suffering will help others!

This is to put the case at its most extreme. Throughout the history of Christendom, there has been a tension between the fundamental and liberal views of the faith. It is the fundamentalist approach that sees the faith in exclusive terms, and leads on to the tribal vision of the elect of God. Liberal Christians, in contrast, from the early years of the Church have sought a broader interpretation of the faith, and have aimed to be inclusive rather than exclusive in their approach to others. In so doing, they have given an emphasis to the faith that renders it supportive of human rights, an emphasis that has played a significant part in the international advance from civic rights to human rights.

Spirituality and Human Rights

Although the relationship of organized religion to human rights has been ambivalent, human rights themselves constitute an authentic and vital component of modern spirituality. According to the argument in Chapter 4, a modern natural theology can be developed pointing to belief in the Creator of a physical universe inhabited by autonomous spiritual beings. The freedom of these autonomous beings, human beings, is a necessity if the created order is to be both interesting and fulfilling to its Creator. This need for freedom leads in turn to the requirement for human rights. Given the limited implementation of human rights on this earth, the argument points finally to the need for life beyond death, for human destiny in eternity, with God the Creator as the ultimate guarantor of human rights and freedom.

This argument is conceptually tidy. Modern spiritual life is characterized by commitments to truth and human rights, and by beliefs in God the Creator and the eternal destiny of humankind. The two behavioural commitments and the two religious beliefs come together in a broad spiritual harmony in which the whole of humankind can participate. This brief summary is consistent, elegant even, and can form the basis of a worthy spiritual aspiration. But problems emerge as soon as one looks a little closer, and they will need serious efforts to overcome. As indicated, the development of human rights has been largely secular. That is to say, the commitment to freedom and human rights has emerged out of the social and political life of nations, rather than their religious institutions. In part, this is because the theistic religions of the world have tended to become associated with tribalism, and in so doing have found it difficult to express truths applicable to the whole of humankind. The commitment to freedom and human rights has developed largely therefore as a component of a secular life, a characteristic that must be recognized in any subsequent association with religious belief.

Together truth and freedom form the first two characteristics of the new thrust in secular spiritual activity. Which comes first? In this text truth has been chosen, but there is really no great significance in the order. Spiritual life can be sought and found today in a purely secular setting, through a commitment to freedom and human rights, however strong the accompanying forces of tribalism, and a commitment to truth, however uncomfortable the particular truths.

As indicated, the commitment to freedom and human rights can be associated entirely rationally with beliefs in God the Creator and in eternal life. But the connection, although rational, is not necessary. This point can be demonstrated in the context of some of the principal clauses of the Universal Declaration of Human Rights.

'No one shall be subjected to torture', says the Universal Declaration. It does not matter what you believe, it does not matter how you have behaved. You should not be tortured. Why should you not be tortured? Because you are a human being.

'No one shall be subjected to arbitrary arrest, detention or exile.' It does not matter who you are, you should not be imprisoned arbitrarily. Why should you not be imprisoned? Because you are a human being.

It is this commitment to behave in particular ways toward all human beings, just because they are human beings, and not because they have certain beliefs or because they have behaved in certain ways that marks out the new form of spirituality that is burgeoning in our time. Why does the mere fact of a person being a human being invoke such a response? In the context of modern spirituality, it is because a human being is recognized first and foremost as a spiritual being, with both spiritual and physical needs. Expressed in more down to earth language, the preamble to the Universal Declaration of Human Rights gives the reason as 'the inherent dignity . . . of all members of the human family', recognition of which is 'the foundation of freedom, justice and peace in the world'. The preamble also speaks of 'the dignity and worth of the human person', and article 1 of the declaration states: 'All human beings are born free and equal in dignity and rights. They are endowed with reason and conscience and should act towards one another in a spirit of brotherhood.' This sense of the dignity and brotherhood of all human beings is an essential element of modern spirituality. Furthermore, it is given expression in a document which is entirely secular. The Universal Declaration of Human Rights says nothing of God, and mentions religion only to affirm the right of each human being to follow and practise the religion of his or her choice. Other documents relating to human rights, those that define the vision and mission of Amnesty International for example, are likewise restricted to statements without a religious content.

Given the history of religion, at least in the western parts of the world, it was certainly desirable and probably inevitable that the development of human rights should have taken place principally in the secular domain. But can it remain like that? Questions about God, creation and eternity will keep crowding in upon the human race, and the answers that are reached strongly influence the way that people behave towards one another. For intellectually convinced humanists, pragmatic statements that simply declare the dignity of man may be all that is needed. For example, there are humanists who belong to organizations such as Amnesty International. They are utterly committed to the cause of human rights, and yet seemingly believe neither in God nor in any life beyond this present one. They are remarkable people and their devotion is very humbling. Many others, however, will not be content with such a position. Instead, they will seek a metaphysical or religious foundation for statements that declare the dignity of humankind and the nature of human rights. Given the current lack of participation in organized religion, this raises serious questions. To what extent, if at all, can the ancient religions be expected to provide the appropriate foundation? Clearly, that is not a question to which there can be any single simple answer. Certainly the liberal elements within the world religions will make their best endeavours, and may achieve a significant measure of success. Indeed, many liberal Christians would probably regard that statement as being too cautious, and would point to the outstanding current involvement of practising Christians in the work of human rights organizations. But sadly the thrust of religious fundamentalism is by no means exhausted, and the tendency to dwell upon the more condemnatory aspects of the biblical texts not only encourages an exclusivist attitude to belief but is almost wholly inimical to the development of human rights.

So what will be needed if the commitment to freedom in modern spirituality is to attain a significant level of coherence in a religion or metaphysics? Will it be a new religion altogether? That is not a likely answer, although it is possible that inter-faith dialogue will lead to a form of religious consensus among the more liberal members of different religions which could take upon itself some of the characteristics of a new faith. What is more likely, however, is that liberalism will continue its growth within the framework of existing religious bodies, albeit with a higher level of cooperation obtaining between them. But whatever the particular outcome, for many people a return to a religious orthodoxy of any kind seems an improbable option. In its absence, some common principles will be needed if modern spiritual life is to be more than merely a matter of individual choice.

For those who hold to belief in God, a common element in modern times could be the idea that the divine Creator of all things and all beings holds a universal concern for the whole of humankind, and has a commitment in eschatological terms to provide a common framework of freedom and human rights for every individual person. To support this notion, an associated metaphysic could begin with the sort of mind/body argument that was offered in Chapter 1, in which it would be emphasized that the mental or spiritual dimension in life is not reducible to the merely physical. Thence the argument could develop to encompass the notion of a created reality that is both interesting and fulfilling to its Creator. Within this created reality, God would endow individual spiritual beings with genuine freedom of thought, belief, decision and action.

The first characteristic of spiritual life in such a universe would be the commitment to follow truth, and to accept the ensuing uncertainties without allowing them to occasion a departure from other aspects of spiritual life. Essential would be the requirement to uphold the rights of all human beings, and to accept that as a moral responsibility over and above any corresponding tribal commitment. The basis would be the recognition that human beings are spiritual beings first, deserving of dignity, and only afterwards members of any particular faith, tribe or group.

The above argument offers the possibility of a common basis for secular spiritual life. It is too limited, however, to provide an adequate theological framework for human rights, although it does offer an outline sketch for such a framework. One of the most basic theological questions is this: are human rights given by God or are they invented by humankind? If it is the former, then, unlike the Ten Commandments they are evidently not given by revelation. They have therefore to be discovered by human endeavour – presumably in a manner broadly analogous to the discovery of God-given scientific laws. Upon that basis, any particular statement of human rights, the Universal Declaration of Human Rights for example, has to be interpreted as a limited expression of the absolute rights conferred by God. What of the alternative possibility? Suppose human rights are not given by God, but are determined by human beings in the exercise of their spiritual autonomy. In that case, they would still need to be confirmed and guaranteed by God, so that they could fulfil their role in eternity. But could that work without limit? Would God endorse any set of rights that humankind might choose? A detailed study of these issues is beyond the scope of this text, and there is no simple way of choosing between the possibilities – perhaps the truth is subtler than either and involves something of each. Whatever the outcome, however, what remains essential is the recognition that freedom and human rights are of fundamental importance in a God-given spiritual realm.

Returning to the immediacy of events on earth, there is a danger that what has been offered is just a little too conceptually tidy, an argument that fails to take sufficient cognizance of the vagaries, ambiguities and uncertainties of life. What are the things that are beyond reasonable doubt in the field of spiritual activity? First, that there has been in Britain over the last two hundred years a significant decline in the level of organized religious activity. Secondly, that there has been a substantial secular development in the commitment to freedom and human rights. (This has happened on an international as well as a national basis.) Thirdly, the decline in religious activity in Britain has led not so much to atheism as to a cautious and doubting theism – a theism based upon a strong commitment to the pursuit of objective truth. As such it is a theism deriving partly from traditional Christian teaching, but partly also from natural theology.

This does not provide a particularly extensive set of facts upon which to build the structure for a modern spiritual life. Nevertheless, it is what there is, and at least one can identify the Universal Declaration of Human Rights and the ensuing growth of supporting organizations such as Amnesty International as constituting authentic markers for a new thrust of spiritual activity. Furthermore, it is a thrust that can be recognized as differing from the spirituality of previous times by its potential applicability to the whole of the human race. Beyond that one can also affirm that, amidst the welter of belief, unbelief and doubt that characterizes the contemporary religious scene, there will be found many individuals who would wish to associate their commitments to truth and freedom with a belief in God. Within that number, however, there will inevitably be those who have parted company with religious orthodoxy. Where that has happened, there must be the danger that beliefs and commitments will be held only piecemeal, and thus become liable to fragmentation under the pressures and difficulties of daily life. What must be hoped is that arguments linking commitments to truth and freedom with beliefs in God and eternal life can provide the newer secular forms of spirituality with sufficient coherence to enable them to overcome such dangers. No doubt there are practising Churchpeople who would regard a return to the pew as a much better answer, but for many people that will remain an unlikely option!

In summary, the foundations of modern spirituality are constituted in the dual commitments to truth and freedom. As such, they mark a radical departure from the spirituality of earlier times. But it must be noted that they are still only the foundations. Truth has to be applied to actual sentences and beliefs, unless it is to remain merely a spiritual abstraction. Freedom likewise is there to provide the opportunity for things to happen. If nothing happens, then freedom is wasted. Next therefore, in these thoughts, must be a consideration of the kind of truths that can be sought and the choice of spiritual activities that can be undertaken, within the framework that freedom and human rights provide.

Notes

1. Larry Siedentop, *Democracy in Europe*, Penguin Books, 2001.
2. Paul Badham, *The Contemporary Challenge of Modernist Theology*, University of Wales Press, 1998.
3. The Universal Declaration of Human Rights. Adopted and proclaimed by the General Assembly of the United Nations on 10 December 1948. The declaration is composed of a preamble and thirty articles. The preamble proclaims the declaration to be a common standard for all peoples and all nations, and article 1 begins its message by asserting that all human beings are born free and equal in dignity and rights.
4. Declaration of Independence. Issued by the American Continental Congress, 1776.
5. John Stuart Mill, *On Liberty*, 1859, J. M. Dent Everyman Library, 1993.
6. John H. Elliott, Dorothy Dymond Memorial Lecture, Portsmouth, 1992.
7. Genesis 17:4–8.
8. John 3:16.
9. Matthew 24:39–41.

6
Caring

Past and Present

It seems a little anti-climactic to begin this chapter with a piece on terminology, but in its absence the result could easily be confusion. Love and kindness, caring and compassion, all these are brought together under the title of 'charity' in the New Testament of the Bible. 'Charity' has a more restricted and particular modern meaning, however, so the term 'love' is often used in its place. 'Love', on the other hand, has acquired a very broad connotation in modern times, extending to romance and physical sexual activity. If a single word is needed in this text to embrace love and kindness, caring and compassion, 'caring' will be used for secular earth bound events, and 'love' for those cases where the theme is more overtly religious. It will not always be an ideal choice, but at least the intent has been declared. At risk of tedium, multiple expressions will often be used, thus avoiding the difficulty.

Commitments to love and kindness, caring and compassion, have always been regarded as vital characteristics of spiritual life, and their significance today is no less profound than it was in earlier times. The importance of freedom in modern secular spirituality has already been declared. Part of its function is to open the door to other relationships and activities. Where spirituality is concerned, love and kindness, caring and compassion, are among the most important. As elements of spiritual life, they occupy a fundamental and indeed primary position, not requiring to be explained or justified by any external reference. They provide their own purposes, they confer their own values, and do not exist just to be a means toward some further or higher goal.

Love not only constitutes an inescapable characteristic of spiritual life; its presence brings modern secular spirituality into close accord with the religious spirituality of previous ages. Love is a central theme of Christianity. Whatever the particular form of Christian doctrine, there is a common belief that Jesus, by his actions and words, gave to human beings a unique expression of love, and through that expression pointed the way toward God. But there remain nevertheless significant differences between the traditional biblical approach to love, and that of modern secular spirituality.

In the modern world, love and caring emerge as elements of a spirituality in which freedom and human rights provide the foundation. In turn, freedom and human rights build upon tolerance, respect, a commitment to human brotherhood and a belief in the essential dignity of every human being. Love, as offered in the Old and New Testaments of the Bible, does not possess the same foundation. The Old Testament is more inclined to emphasize man's disobedience than his dignity. No sooner are brothers introduced than Cain slays Abel. Even in the New Testament very little is to be found about the brotherhood of all people. Love is presented directly, without any progression through tolerance and respect. It may be argued that where people love and care for one another, then, *a fortiori*, they will also tolerate and respect each other. But whilst this provides an answer in the conceptual sense, it does not always work well in practice. Both traditional Christian spirituality and modern secular spirituality embrace love and caring, but the approaches are substantially different, and it will not help to think otherwise.

Turning specifically to the modern secular understanding of love and caring, there are a number of problems. Of these, three are of particular importance, and will constitute the subject matter of the immediately ensuing sections. They are *tribalism*, *competition* and *esteem*. All three impact profoundly upon love and caring. Their influence will be explored in this chapter, which will then seek to establish the position that love and caring occupy today in the wider frame of spiritual life.

Tribal Responsibilities

As previously discussed, the actual ideas of freedom and human rights, as well as their implementation, struggled for many years to make progress in an environment where tribalism occupied a dominant position. Not unexpectedly, it transpires that caring is also profoundly influenced by tribalism, but in a subtly different way.

Because love builds today upon the foundation of the dignity and rights of every human being, it acquires characteristics of tolerance and acceptance that had to struggle for recognition in earlier times. This is not to deny that love in a close-knit community is often expressed through the discharge of those particular responsibilities that are associated with membership. But it is to accept that charity can never be wholly contained within any group or tribal boundary, and that those outside a community should never be excluded from the concept of care. Nor does the argument finish there. Caring is not limited even to the totality of humankind. Modern spirituality needs to be characterized by a concern and compassion that extends to all living creatures.

Attractive as the argument above may seem, it is also comprehensively idealistic. Offered without qualification, it may present insuperable difficulties in implementation. An immediate problem is the size of the world, or, more precisely, the size of its human population. How is it possible for any one person, however devoted and well meaning, to be a friend to all the world? Confronted, for example, with a famine affecting a million people, what is there in practice that a solitary person can do? The answer must be to use tribalism as a positive force. One person alone may be able to contribute too little to make a difference, except to a very few out of the suffering million. But one person as part of his or her 'tribe' (whether 'tribe' is the nation or some other corporate body) may be able to contribute to an organized 'tribal' response on a scale that is able to measure up to the problem. In this way, tribalism fulfils its elementary function of enabling individuals collectively to do what would be beyond the capacity of individuals acting separately. That is an obvious enough point, but not a trivial one. There are many circumstances in which it can apply. It leaves the idealism of caring untouched, however, and touches only part of the problem.

More serious is an issue exemplified by some remarks addressed to me by the husband and father of a particularly close-knit family. Talking about the nature of family commitments, he commented: 'If you are on a sinking ship, the first thing that you do is put your own child in the lifeboat. After that, you have choices. You may put someone else's child in the lifeboat, or you may climb in yourself. But you have no choice about what you do first!'

The position the father was enunciating might not command universal support, but what he said would be true for many people. The family is perhaps the smallest group of persons that falls within the definition of tribe. Within that group, there are particular responsibilities of care that often outweigh other wider considerations. The commitment to love has therefore to be interpreted and implemented within the framework of family responsibilities. It is the family, constituted as a tribe, that sets the priorities.

A similar argument applies to many other tribal groups. In time of war, the commitment of love and care may require a person to give up life itself in the service of the nation. Furthermore, the nature of military service is such that a person may be called upon to kill other human beings. Tribal priorities impact massively upon love and caring, determining priorities in ways that may involve not only the commitment of life itself but also the taking of life itself. The issue of war will be looked at again in Chapter 8. At this point, it is being picked out in order to give a particularly vivid example of the manner in which tribal responsibilities can impact upon human commitments to care and to love. Tribal responsibilities do not invalidate the claim to attach fundamental spiritual importance to caring, but they do profoundly influence the manner in which that commitment can be implemented. A general call to love others, a call that pays no heed to the responsibilities of tribal membership, is at risk of being not so much idealistic as unrealistic. In modern secular spirituality, the argument flows in two directions. Love and caring are profoundly influenced in one direction by the obligation to uphold human rights, and in the other by the requirement to take heed of the demands of tribalism. The outcome can be complex, particularly in terms of priorities, and in consequence modern spiritual life is liable to manifest itself in forms some distance removed from those that a straightforward declaration of love and caring might suggest.

Competition

There is no escaping the competitive nature of humankind. As an assertion, that is perhaps a mild exaggeration. Some religious teaching tries not to notice the thrust to compete, and finds itself sharing the myopia with certain minority forms of educational and political thinking. But most people most of the time recognize the force of competition in human affairs, and in this text there is certainly no intention to underplay its importance. Competition is both direct and vicarious; it can be either individual or tribal. The whole vast business of professional sport testifies to the human capacity to enjoy vicarious competition. Why does it matter that one group of highly paid young men whom a supporter has never met personally should win a football match against another group of highly paid young men whom he or she has also never met personally? The reality is that it does! A heady mixture of tribalism and competition drives the emotions, and a high proportion of the human race appears to succumb.

Sport of all kinds is competition both stylized and formalized. Competition in business and employment is often less formal, but it can become as fierce or even fiercer. In this respect, the whole international structure of capitalism and free markets is built very largely upon the notion that human activity is essentially competitive, not just competitive on occasions. Finally, when it comes to war, competition reaches its peak, with large-scale killing by offensive action accepted as a legitimate competitive activity.

Why is competition so important in human affairs? The answer is likely to be many faceted, but one important point is that biological existence as a whole is highly competitive. Even plants struggle for their place in the sun, and within the animal kingdom competition is present in virtually every activity. Predators and their prey are in a state of relentless competition. Where progression is concerned, the continued existence of a species may be secured by having the males struggle with one another, sometimes to the death, for the opportunity to mate with the females. 'Survival of the fittest' equates to competition of one form or another to discover who is the fittest. So if human beings exhibit a powerful desire to compete, they do it at least partly because they belong to the totality of biological life.

Why is biological life so essentially competitive? It is difficult to know. As a contrasting point, it can be properly remarked that cooperation is also strongly evident in the natural order. But even though competition is only one of the defining characteristics of biological life, what is undeniable is that its presence still puts serious question marks against the belief that God is love. It is one thing to look at the world, to wonder at the world, and to be drawn to the belief that God the Creator must be both omnipotent and omniscient. It is quite another to look at the violent strivings of living creatures, one against another, and to sustain the belief that God is love. Where animals are concerned, the point was made vividly and forcefully in the poem by William Blake:

Tiger, tiger, burning bright,
In the forests of the night,
What immortal hand or eye
Could frame thy fearful symmetry?[1]

How does one believe that God who created the tiger is also full of caring and compassion towards its prey? There is no obvious answer. The argument is sometimes offered that animals are not aware beings, have no feelings, and therefore do not suffer. For many people, that is not a solution that seems credible. Does it nevertheless make too much of the circumstances of animals? Some will certainly think so. Perhaps the issue is one of autonomy. Perhaps the preventing of competition among the creatures of the earth would lead logically to an outcome that would interfere too much with spiritual freedom. Again, it is difficult to know.

The issue remains in doubt. The natural order of living things, the competitive strivings and consequential sufferings of both human beings and animals constitute a continuing cause of religious uncertainty. It will not go away, and it can place a persistent question mark against the capacity to believe in a caring and compassionate God. As previously remarked in Chapter 4, there is no ready escape into a pessimistic theology, as that leads in effect though not in words to a form of polytheism. A satisfactory answer, if such can be found, would certainly require a belief in eternity and perhaps also an expectation of eschatological change. To balance the argument, however, and to be consistent with the previous points, it needs to be added that even the most persistent of doubts is not the same as a disbelief.

Returning to the consideration of competition among human beings, as distinct from animals, competition itself is not necessarily inimical to love or to the belief in God as a God of love. However, it most certainly raises questions, and there are no easy answers. To make progress, the issue needs to be unpacked and examined case by case. To this end, the particularly significant issue of competition in professional life will be looked at in some detail in Chapter 8. Suffice it to say at this point that the more ruthless aspects of competition will often be sinful, militating directly against caring and compassion. But that does not provide for the notional elimination of all competition on moral grounds, even supposing such a notion to be remotely credible, which it is not. What has to be recognized is that the commitment to caring and love needs to be sustained alongside the satisfaction of the competitive drive. The latter forms an essential element of the *thymotic* nature of many human beings. It cannot simply be dismissed as wickedness, something to be written out of life, and this applies notwithstanding the fact that many of its individual manifestations are clearly wicked, or include wicked components. Just how a synthesis of caring and competition can be managed philosophically is not clear. The attempt will be made, in Chapter 8, to work toward a synthesis in certain individual cases. Beyond that the best that can be offered is the hopeful prediction that a universal synthesis will ultimately emerge, a thought predicated, albeit cautiously, upon the dual beliefs in God the Creator and in eternity.

Esteem – The Value of the Person

The esteem in which Dick and Harry hold Tom is the value that they attach to him as a person. There is also the esteem in which Tom holds himself, his self-esteem or sense of self-worth, and finally there is the esteem in which God holds Tom. There is a certain reluctance to use the term 'esteem' in respect of God, the term 'value' being often preferred. The reason for this choice may lie with the question of intrinsic value. Does Tom have an intrinsic value as a person, a value that may or may not equate with his self-esteem or the esteem in which Dick and Harry hold him? Could Tom, Dick and Harry all be in error? The assumption is that God will not be in error, so that the value he attributes to Tom is the actual or intrinsic value. Alternatively, a believer might apply the converse, and say that the idea of intrinsic value is only meaningful if regarded as the value given by God. This is all a bit theoretical, but it is useful to be as clear as possible about terms and ideas before putting them into action!

As remarked in Chapter 2, the value of a person is multifaceted. When it comes to esteem, this too can apply to the various aspects of a person, his or her personal qualities, including morality, wealth, power and physical attributes. But whichever aspect of a person is under consideration, the actual desire to be esteemed is always *thymotic*, and must not be confused with desires that arise from instinct or appetite. In his penetrating analysis of human development, Francis Fukuyama identifies the *thymotic* need for esteem as the single most important motivator of social and political activity. As noted in Chapter 2, he distinguishes the desire to enjoy equal esteem or to be of the same value as other persons, from the desire to enjoy greater esteem or to be of greater value than other persons. Whilst the former can lead to acts of love and caring, the latter can result in the exact opposite. Indeed, according to Fukuyama, many of the world's most dreadful iniquities can be laid at the door of an excessive desire for superior recognition.[2]

It would be difficult to fault Fukuyama's approach. Certainly human beings are united in feeling the need for recognition, the need to be valued. An inferiority complex, an absence of a sense of self-worth, can be desperately damaging. A colleague visiting a large office complex remarked to me that virtually every office in the building housed a manager, a supervisor, or a chief 'something-or-other'. The prolific use of such terms testified to the innate requirement for human beings to acquire esteem, in this instance the esteem of occupying a named managerial position. In similar vein, the wearing of uniforms or robes, or the acquiring of honours or office, all testify to the desire for status which is found in almost every walk of life. Examples could be multiplied, but it is hardly necessary. The case is just too strong to need extended exposition.

There are questions to be raised, however, about the wisdom of dividing the wish for esteem between equality and superiority. The problem lies in the need for measurement. Although a person may initially think in terms of equal value, once the idea of seeing a particular value in comparative terms has taken root, it is often tempting to proceed from the desire for equality to the desire for something more than equality. Egalitarianism may seem morally idealistic, but it may not be helpful to press it as a desirable feature of social and political systems. Esteem does not have to be commensurable, and the alternative approach is to stress the unique value of each individual human being, a value not to be measured or compared but to be appreciated and enjoyed for its own particular and distinct characteristic.

That may sound reasonable, but if left without further comment it must also constitute something of an evasion. The combination of human competitive nature with the need for esteem all too easily leads towards megalomania. It is a tendency widespread in humankind, and cannot simply be dismissed, minimized or discounted. What is also undeniable is that love, as expressed by St Paul for example, has wholly different characteristics. 'Charity', we are told, 'is not puffed up.'[3] Megalomania, on the other hand, most certainly is! The task of admitting competition and the need for self-esteem without simultaneously denying love is never going to be easy. But neither will it be sufficient merely to dismiss competition and esteem as undesirable elements of human nature, and assume that they must simply be removed in order to follow a spiritual path. A subtler version of the same problem is found in the Beatitudes. According to Jesus, the meek are blessed, and will inherit the earth. It is not impossible for a person to possess a strong sense of self-esteem and yet remain humble and meek, but it is not something that will come to pass without serious spiritual travail. Hard it may be, but the complex nature of love and caring in a modern spiritual setting will only be properly grasped when the issues of competition and esteem are brought adequately to the fore.

The Heart of Spiritual Life

As previously argued, the first two characteristics of modern secular spirituality are the commitments to seek truth and to uphold freedom. Both are important in themselves, but they are also important in establishing a framework within which deeper forms of spiritual life can be sought. We need to affirm what is true and grasp the opportunities provided by freedom in order that we can then do 'such-and-such'. But what exactly is the spiritual 'such-and-such'? The answer, or at least part of the answer, lies in the practice of love and kindness, of caring and compassion. As previously remarked, they occupy a primary position among the components of a modern spiritual life. They do not require justification by some external reference, but constitute their own purposes, and do not therefore exist only as a step toward some further or higher goal. Alongside them, however, are the pressures of tribalism, competition and esteem. None of them are necessarily inimical to love and caring, but any or all are liable to intrude and can lead to quite different goals and choices of action. If love and caring are adopted as primary goals of secular spirituality, then their individual expressions will have to be worked out, person by person, in the context of tribal commitments, the wish to compete and the need for a sense of self-worth.

These are not the only problems. Love and caring inevitably raise issues that go beyond the affairs of this world. However much we love people in this world, the ending is always in sadness. Death separates us, and there is nothing that we can do on this earth to prevent it happening. This does not dissuade people from loving one another, and for those who have no belief whatsoever in a further life, the knowledge of their mortal nature adds an urgency and poignancy to the relationship. But for many, there is the hope if not the actual belief that this world is not the sum of human existence and that love in some vital way is carried beyond this world into the next.

It is important to recognize the sequence of the argument in modern thought. Because we love one another dearly, we hope for a reunion in another world. Orthodox Christians relate this hope to the sacrifice of Jesus. Those who have departed from orthodoxy or never acquired it can still hold to the reasonable argument that love will only triumph if carried beyond the shocks and changes of this present life. Persons recognizing such an argument can hope that it is indeed God's purpose in creation that love shall ultimately triumph. There can be no guarantees, but it does belong to modern spirituality to take caring as a fundamental characteristic, and to do so in the hope or belief that it is not wholly limited to the chances of this temporal life.

Is this the finish? Modern secular spirituality is now defined in terms of three commitments, these being to seek for truth, to uphold the right to freedom of every human being and to practice the care of others. These commitments have been put into the metaphysical context of beliefs in God the Creator and the prospect of eternal life. For many people, these beliefs will be accompanied by a significant element of doubt, even to the extent that hope rather than belief may be the more appropriate description. Nevertheless, given the commitments, the beliefs and the doubts, all set out in some detail, is there anything else that needs to be said?

The answer is that further difficulties remain. First, throughout these remarks, the question of sin has been touched upon but lightly, and that will not suffice. Talk of truth, freedom and love is merely idealistic if the vast extent of human moral failure remains overlooked. An endeavour will be made to explore this forbidding issue in the next chapter.

Following this exploration and closely associated with it must come the issue of the practicalities of life, as distinct from the generalities with which the earlier parts of this text have been chiefly composed. There is nothing wrong with offering generalities, but life is composed of actual people engaged in actual events. In Chapter 8, some of the realities and particularities will be identified, in an attempt to flesh out the abstractions and generalities of earlier thoughts. With the exploration of the secular concluded, the argument will turn in Chapter 9 to overtly religious matters, exploring how far if at all these ideas can be related to Christian religious orthodoxy. Attention will also be paid to the presence of the other great religions in contemporary British society. Finally, in Chapter 10, an endeavour will be made to say something of relevance concerning the great themes of eternity and creativity. Clearly, ideas of creativity are necessary for belief in God the Creator. But, as first suggested in Chapter 1, the creative (or destructive) nature of decision-making is also fundamental to human mental being. In Chapter 10, the spiritual significance of creativity will be explored in relation to the ultimate destiny of humankind.

Notes

1. William Blake, *The Tiger*, Songs of Experience, 1794.
2. Francis Fukuyama, *The End of History and the Last Man*, Penguin Books, 1992.
3. 1 Corinthians 13:4–5.

7

Reconciliation

The Presence of Evil

Evil occasions the most terrible suffering among humankind, and raises fundamental spiritual problems. Its malign presence is so powerful in human affairs that it is regarded by some as putting serious questions marks against the nature or even the being of God, and it leads on to create elemental divisions in philosophy and religious belief. The initial question is in itself quite simple. If God is omnipotent and good, how did evil arise? Answers tend not to be so simple!

As already indicated in Chapter 4, one positive response is embodied in what Jonathan Clatworthy has called an optimistic theology.[1] In that account, the optimistic response to evil is to insist that the almighty and loving God always remains in complete control, that evil is only able to arise because God grants human beings the capacity for moral choice, and that ultimately the benefits of moral freedom will outweigh any deleterious consequences of individuals making the wrong choice. Upon that argument, God never wills that a human being should sin, but permits it in order that each human being should have the opportunity for moral development.

In contrast, pessimistic theologies find sufficient cause in the presence of evil to give up the notion that God remains in complete control and that all can be redeemed. In its place comes the acceptance that God has his rivals, that we live in a world of moral strife, and that whilst God will ultimately triumph, he will do so only to the extent of destroying his enemies or dispatching them to hell. He will not ultimately achieve any form of reconciliation with them. God provides an objective standard of goodness, but the world does not live up to it. There is an element of evil built into the way things are!

A third possibility is to abandon belief, not in God himself, but in the holiness of God. In this option, God creates the universe, but its evident moral imperfection mirrors the imperfection of its creator. Clearly this position contrasts with both optimistic and pessimistic theologies, which are at least agreed that God constitutes the origin of moral standards. If God is less than perfect, however, no single authoritative source for morality can be found. As such, this option is best described as a morally neutral theology.

The remaining options are those of agnosticism and atheism. Agnosticism constitutes a powerful ongoing uncertainty as to whether there is a God – so powerful that the uncertainty itself becomes the dominant theme. Atheism tips over into the certainty, or at least the confident belief, that there is no God. Although logically distinct, they share the characteristic of leaving divine activity outside the equation. It follows that freedom, morality, life itself, all have to be considered without the presence of God. It may be recalled that earlier, in Chapter 4, two different possibilities were explored for the origin of the physical universe. Either it was created, and thus had a Creator, or it just happened – it was the product of 'happenstance'. In the earlier argument, the exploration was in favour of a created universe, although not without a tinge of doubt, but that was before any consideration of evil. For some people, the inability to find a satisfactory way of relating a holy Creator to an imperfect world pushes the scales back in the direction of agnosticism or atheism. For the agnostic and the atheist, no single authoritative source of moral standard is to be found, just the separate beliefs of individuals.

What can be said about these five options? Those for whom the state of the natural order is already a source of doubt will find an even greater element of uncertainty in the pervading presence of evil. Not many, however, will be drawn into the morally neutralist camp. This tends to be a practical as much as a philosophic thing. It is simply not apparent how human beings could respond to an imperfect God, or be at all clear about the character of the imperfections. Atheism is likewise limited in its appeal. Confident assertions of disbelief or unbelief are not easily derived even from the worst examples of human sin. Neither option can be formally dismissed, but in this text it is not intended to pursue either of them in any further detail.

In addition and as previously indicated in Chapter 4, there is no great argument to be found in favour of pessimistic theologies. Because their implications are polytheistic, their metaphysics are vague – particularly their accounts of the origin of existence. Much more seriously, however, at the personal and social level their pessimism is often applied to other people – those outside the tribal frontier that separates true believers from the rest. At its worst, the pessimistic idea of the separation of the saved and the damned encourages the construction of macabre images of hell and eternal torment. Feeding off selected verses from Revelation, the most extreme of such theologies not only support the idea of hell, but also advance the notion that the saved shall benefit by being permitted a view of the tortures of the damned.[2] When pessimistic beliefs of that kind are put forward, it is difficult to envisage any limit to the sufferings that could be inflicted (on this earth) upon those supposedly outside the circle of the elect. Today, of course, these more extreme forms of belief have become rare, but they remain within the span of pessimistic theologies, and a possible resurgence can never be wholly discounted.

Having dismissed so many of the alternatives, it follows if only upon negative grounds that this argument must remain at least loosely attached to an optimistic theology, with an occasional tendency to desert it in the direction of agnosticism. That is to be minimalist. As indicated before, the optimistic argument, expressed so clearly by Clatworthy, does have an appeal and a rationale that are lacking in its alternatives. It is a position that needs further analysis, however, in the working out of the implications of freedom. From a logical standpoint, it is difficult to see how God can remain in complete control if he grants genuine moral freedom to the spiritual beings that he creates. As previously discussed, the problem is akin to God making a stone so big that he cannot throw it away! Of course, one could argue that God can make people perfectly free today, but punish them tomorrow if they behave badly! Taken to its extreme, however, this argument heads back in the direction of heaven and hell and unredeemed evil. So if a return to pessimism and the invention of a rival god are to be avoided, then the optimistic answer to the presence of wickedness will need a further and more thorough explanation.

Stemming from previous deliberations in Chapter 4, the approach taken focuses yet again on the purpose and nature of freedom. What use is a spiritual being that has no freedom? Is he or she still a spiritual being in any serious sense? It is not difficult to program a computer to say, 'I love you', but is there any value in the exercise? Freedom is essential if spiritual beings are to be able to love and care for one another, and if the universe is to be of interest and value to its Creator. The creating of free spiritual beings is therefore an essential part of the process of creation. Once free spirits have been created, however, it becomes a logical impossibility to declare that the omnipotence of God requires that he remain in complete control. It is a misunderstanding of omnipotence to think that he could do any such thing. Free spirits are free to love and care for others, but they are also free to turn against their fellow spirits and to engage in a whole range of activities that are held to be wicked. To be precise about the implications of freedom, it is not so much that God permits evil as that logically he cannot prevent it, if spiritual beings are to be genuinely free. Because individuals are free, the possibility that they choose evil cannot be ruled out. But it does not follow that the choice of evil leads to a greater good. The fact that God cannot prevent free moral agents from choosing evil does not mean that he ever wills that they should do such a thing, nor does it mean that the outcome can ever be better than it would have been had they chosen otherwise. An evil act is an evil act is an evil act! The person who commits it is redeemable, but the act is a matter of fact, a matter of history, and existence can never be the better because of it. If theological optimism is to be sustained, therefore, it must be done in a way that accepts this stronger interpretation of freedom, and confronts the problem of evil on correspondingly stricter terms.

Law and Love

Theological problems are not the only ones occasioned by the presence of evil. With moral questions, a fundamental difficulty arises due to the fact that the consciences of different human beings tell them different things. Of course, it is also true that people do not always heed their consciences, but that is a separate issue. For the moment let us hold to the point that different consciences say different things to their owners. In part, these differences relate to different circumstances and experiences. Of these, the situations with regard to tribe seems to be the most significant. During the terrible conflict in Bosnia during the 1990s, for example, the most appalling deeds were performed without the perpetrators appearing to believe that what they were doing was morally wrong. There may have been cases in which conscience was being ignored in the heat of the moment, but that was far from the whole explanation. It seemed that the most important feature in the framing of moral responses was the commitment to tribe. Consciences pointed toward one mode of conduct toward members of the same tribe, and a quite different mode to members of others. Tribalism may not be the only source of distinction between different moral codes, but it is clearly a most compelling one.

There is, however, evidence of a positive response to this last problem. Whilst the last century witnessed the most dreadful excesses of tribalism, it also experienced the gradual but broadly based development of the commitment to human rights. Although the idea of a common code of morality delivering human rights to every human being took root but slowly, it did take root and is now becoming firmly established, at least among the liberal democracies of the world. There is also a growing realisation that criminal law, both national and international, should constitute the reverse side of the coin of freedom and human rights. Justice delivers rights, and to do so it requires a moral code and a set of laws expressive of that code. The wider the acceptance of human rights, therefore, the greater the formal commonalty of human conscience.

According to the non-theist view, there is no moral authority beyond the individual conscience, and individual consciences say different things. It follows that human rights, the idea of a common moral code and a consequential set of commonly accepted laws, offer a pragmatic challenge to the neutralist position, a challenge that rests upon the capacity of human beings to come together in pursuit of a common moral stance. For the theist, however, the outcome is different. Neither the optimistic nor the pessimistic positions, as previously outlined, will easily fit. As previously explored in Chapter 5, a common position on human rights might be thought of as a position to which humankind is inevitably drawn, because those are the rights that God the Creator always intended should ultimately obtain. Alternatively, a common position might be obtained as a consequence of the exercise of moral autonomy, with the outcome endorsed by the Creator but not willed by him. All this might seem somewhat esoteric, but it is a point that touches once again upon the very nature of freedom. In the absence of a new revelation, however, it is not an issue to which there is likely to be an early solution! Whatever the outcome, however, human rights and an associated common moral code will remain of fundamental spiritual importance in the response to evil.

A further issue concerns the relationship between love and law, or between caring and morality. Loving activity is not necessarily the same thing as morally lawful activity. A person can behave in a morally correct manner, a manner that accords with the moral law, without necessarily being loving and kind, caring and compassionate. The distinction is important, and goes back to the original insistence that *thymos* is not just conscience, but 'heart' as well. Another way of putting it is that conscience cannot reasonably be expanded to include the impetus to loving activity as well as morally lawful activity. The distinction between the two is important, and needs to be sustained in order to avoid the risk of spiritual confusion. A similar argument applies to the ideas of good and evil. There is a tendency to think that if something is not good, then it must be bad, and vice versa. But that oversimplifies the argument. If something is bad, it offends against a moral code. If the moral code is once again observed, then whatever was bad is removed. But that is all. It does not follow that the situation is now good. It may be, but that is another question. Between good and evil there exists a zone of righteousness, in which moral rules are observed, but love and compassion are not necessarily in evidence.

The upholding of moral rules is related to the issue of coercion. A moral code having been established, individuals can be obliged to maintain it, and can be obliged by the use of force. This happens at the national level, where the law of the land is imposed by the police with the authority of the courts to support them. Of course, the law does not deal only in moral issues, and even where it does it cannot be equated directly with individual morality. Nevertheless, national criminal law is expected to be broadly in harmony with individual ideas of morality, and there is likely to be serious trouble if it is not!

But what would happen if an attempt were made to extend the law in the direction of love and caring. Imagine a country with a king who is an absolute monarch. The king becomes distressed at the sight of beggars starving in the city streets, and resolves to take action. He decrees that all his subjects are henceforward to give to beggars on demand, and are liable to execution if they fail. At first no one believes the decree, but after the first few ungenerous (or imprudent) citizens have been executed, the begging community suddenly becomes the subject of instant gifts and rapidly increasing wealth. The king, talking to a visiting emissary, remarks that there is now no country in the whole of the earth that is so marked by its charity and compassion to those in need. There is no need to expand upon the implications of this rather absurd fantasy. The solitary point to draw from it is that love cannot be coerced, and becomes a mere caricature of itself if the attempt is made.

A clear distinction then is found between those matters that fall within a moral code and those that can only voluntarily be adopted. Love and kindness, caring and compassion, these all belong in the latter camp. They can be sought, encouraged and warmly reciprocated, but they cannot be imposed or commanded. The reason is found in the nature of freedom. It is obedience to the moral law that provides the freedom within which love can be sought and given – or withheld if that is the choice. The upholding of the moral law guarantees freedom, but there is no succeeding guarantee that the freedom thus obtained will be used to promote love. All that can be certain is the opportunity!

To avoid possible confusion, it may be worth adding a comment about the distinction between service and caring. In professional activities, for example, there is a subtle distinction between the services that members provide for their wages and the caring that they freely and additionally offer. It is a subtlety that is often difficult to discern, particularly in what are termed 'caring professions', because individuals do not usually seek that kind of employment except with deliberate caring intent. It is much easier to pick out the distinction from the opposite end of the occupational spectrum. A slave can be compelled to serve, but can never be compelled to care!

The Necessity for Reconciliation

Whatever the outcome of the philosophic and intellectual arguments about evil, one thing at least is as clear as it is wretched. Evil abounds. It does so internationally and it does so locally, to the extent that it is not difficult to be gloomy about the whole state of human affairs. At least, in England's green and pleasant land, the more elementary of human rights and freedoms are usually respected and upheld, although in the wake of 11 September 2001 even that statement needs viewing with caution. But elsewhere there are parts of the world where human rights are terribly trampled upon, and even the most elementary of freedoms are denied. 'Ethnic cleansing' is a new and horrible expression in our language. Often women still lack emancipation, and there are places where children are compelled to work from an early age in denial of their childhood. And although the issue may seem less acute, excesses in the desire for economic wealth remain widespread in a world dominated by free market economics and capitalism. The point is not that free markets and the deployment of capital for gain are wrong in themselves, but rather that they make few moral demands, and thus leave the way open for huge excesses in desire. Is a spiritual response possible within such a situation, or are things generally so bad that spiritual life has to be conceived as a disengagement from the modern world? In other words, has the attempt to establish a secular spirituality foundered on the rock of human wickedness? Must spirituality return to the religious cloister (real or metaphorical) to which it once was thought to belong? Upon what spiritual basis, is it appropriate or even possible to confront evil?

At one level, an answer has already been proffered in the recognition that freedom and human rights are essential elements of modern secular spirituality. If human rights are upheld, by the deployment of force if necessary, then many of the more terrible consequences of evil can be prevented or at least mitigated. But whilst that is an essential component of an answer, it is also manifestly incomplete. Spirituality involves relationships – between human beings and between human beings and God. Upholding human rights may limit the harm occasioned by evil, but cannot in itself restore damaged or broken relationships. If spirituality is to grow, then the restoration of relations becomes a vital element. So is there a second component of the answer to wickedness, a component that goes beyond the delivery of freedom and human rights? In fact, there is, and it does retain engagement with the secular world. Furthermore, it is familiar and even straightforward, although not at all comfortable. It is the call to reconciliation, a call to bring together the actions of forgiveness and repentance, in response to those occasions when human relations have become mired by the dominance of evil.

In this country, ideas of repentance and forgiveness tend to be expressed in the language of Christianity, but of course no single religion has a monopoly upon reconciliation (or a monopoly upon truth, freedom or caring). People of any or no beliefs may choose to forgive, and may do so whether the offences are large or small. Nevertheless, not only are the ideas of repentance and forgiveness located in the Christian faith, they have also been given a position of utter and fundamental importance by that faith, a position not readily to be found elsewhere. Furthermore, in this country, if a person recognizes the need to be reconciled as being a crucial part of his or her spiritual life, it will usually happen as a consequence of an early acquaintance with Christian thinking. But whilst the origins of the commitment to reconciliation are often Christian, contemporary understanding is likely to be very different from that of a previous age. Sadly, whilst the Christian faith attaches a fundamental importance to reconciliation, it does so in a manner that has become largely incomprehensible or unacceptable to a great many people. How is it that such a situation has arisen?

The first part of the problem is tribalism. The need for evil doings of the past to be overcome, and for perpetrators and victims alike to make a fresh start, is apparent both at the community and at the individual level. But whilst Christianity, and indeed all the principal religions that draw inspiration from the Old Testament, are concerned with the reconciliation of man with God, their tribal associations have often served to stimulate conflict between human beings rather than resolve it. In Northern Ireland, it has been the inability of Catholic and Protestant Christians to be reconciled to one another that has resulted in an environment of sectarian violence, and in Bosnia it was largely the memory of earlier religious and ethnic warfare that sustained the bleak and unforgiving conflict between Christians and Muslims.

But the problem is not simply or chiefly that of religious tribalism. At the individual level, there are critical issues that stem from the manner in which today's perception of the world differs from that of previous ages. In Britain today the idea of making a ritual sacrifice of an animal in order to propitiate the Almighty is regarded as both primitive and repugnant. It is not simply that the practice has largely vanished, nor even that it is no longer considered to be effectual. Beyond either of those practical considerations, it also seems morally unsound to think that the imposition of a ghastly death upon some helpless creature can somehow rectify a person's misdeeds. But it is that idea, extended to human beings, that forms an important element of the Christian understanding of the redeeming sacrifice of Jesus. He is described as the Paschal Lamb, the perfect sacrifice for the sins of the world. And in developing this idea, Christians follow the Old Testament belief in a God of judgement who must be persuaded by sacrifice to stay his wrathful hand.

Jesus, of course, unlike any actual lamb, made his own choice, and it would be a very hard heart that was not moved by his extraordinary courage and conviction. But responding to his suffering, courage and conviction does not of itself resolve the question of how reconciliation can be viewed in a world that is so very different from the one of biblical times. However greatly individuals may come to value reconciliation, they will not ordinarily see it as depending upon a vicarious act of oblation or satisfaction.

To cite a modern example, a few years ago, a member of a professional football team had both of his legs broken in what was described by the press as a most appalling foul tackle. The next day, a reporter visited the injured player in hospital and asked him if he could ever bring himself to forgive the man who had committed the foul. As subsequently reported, the player replied: 'There is too much bitterness in football already. If he asks me to forgive him, I shall.'

The reply provides a modern paradigm of forgiveness. It revealed an attitude that could lead on to genuine reconciliation, and demanded no separate act of oblation.

Part of the problem is the association of reconciliation with earlier and primitive ideas of justice. In biblical times, monarchs exercised an authority that was not far removed from absolute, and judgement was assumed to be a natural part of their function. They could reward their friends and punish their enemies – and the punishments were often savage. Since God was a King above kings, He could bestow even greater rewards (heaven) and inflict even greater punishments (hell). Biblical thinking of course was far removed from the notions of democratic rule and an independent judiciary. There was little appreciation of the fact that revenge, as a component of justice, neither constituted the noblest of motives nor formed a necessary part of reconciliation. In consequence, early interpretations of Jesus' sacrifice were based on ideas of justice that have ceased to connect with much of the thinking of the modern world.

As a result of this lack of connection, it would appear that many people today have not so much rejected Christian teaching as found it based on ways of thought far removed from their own. Back in the 1960s there was a flurry of activity associated with attempts to demythologize the biblical message and thus render it more relevant to our times. John Robinson created a considerable stir with *Honest to God*, and subsequently speculated about the likelihood of a new reformation for the Church.[3] But looking back at those endeavours, it seems that the religious problem today is not chiefly that of distinguishing between reality and myth in the Bible. It is much more the need to obtain a straightforward grasp of the spiritual importance of reconciliation – a grasp that does not depend upon ways of thinking belonging to an age so far removed from our own.

Reconciliation and Spirituality

In seeking a modern concept of spirituality, it is important not to imagine that the combination of sin plus reconciliation can issue forth in a form of spiritual life that is somehow superior to the life that would have obtained without the sin in the first place. Reconciliation needs to be thought of as the road to recovery, not to fulfilment! That point being made, it is equally important not in any way to discount the role of reconciliation, when evil has wrought its damage to spiritual relations. In the absence of reconciliation, spirituality will either attach itself to a pessimistic theology or else become merely idealistic with little grip upon the harsher realities of life. From the biblical account, it seems that this was a feature of life about which Jesus and his followers were fully aware. Indeed, it can be argued that what should most strongly characterize the religion stemming from the life of Jesus is the recognition that in a sinful world the total commitment to reconciliation is essential for spiritual life. What a sad irony it is that the expression of that commitment in terms of propitiatory sacrifice has unintentionally shrouded the message for a large part of the present generation. Somehow, the whole sense of the utter importance of reconciliation needs to be recovered from the idea of vicarious sacrifice, and made available for the secular spiritual life of the modern world. Reconciliation is not a uniquely Christian virtue, but the absolute nature of that commitment is uniquely Christian. The call for that total commitment, confused though it may have become, remains the distinctively Christian message for the world, a message that must be heeded if an effective form of modern spirituality is to be established.

It would be arrogant to suggest that there is anything original in the above thoughts. Problems with the doctrines of substitutionary atonement are well ventilated. Moreover, liberal Christians have frequently sought alternative interpretations for Jesus' life and work. In so doing they have tended to focus more broadly upon his message and inspirational life. Probably the most significant feature of this argument is the emphasis upon a secular arena for the delivery of the message of reconciliation. Given that context, it may perhaps be helpful to apply to reconciliation those patterns of human thought that have been mainly responsible for the advance of modern life. In any substantial ontology of life will be found persons, events and principles. (A substantial ontology will often include more, but these three will suffice for the purpose.) It belongs to traditional Christianity to focus upon the first two. Thus the Apostle's Creed spells out who the person of Jesus is, and then proclaims the principal events in which he was involved. Principles are not mentioned. In similar vein, it is not uncommon for evangelical Christians to approach a problem by asking what Jesus would have done. With that approach, a course of action is determined not by making reference to underlying principles but by looking at the person of Jesus and trying to decide what choice he would have made. In practice, the tendency will be for the principles to emerge indirectly from the assumptions about Jesus and his choice of action. Outside the fairly tightly drawn circle of evangelical Christians, however, modern individuals are more accustomed to basing their activities directly upon principle. In part, this derives from the successes of science and technology, which are almost wholly based on principle (or law). It also arises from the thrust of modern education, where the espousal of principle is often regarded as a self-evident virtue. Expressing the absolute nature of the Christian commitment to reconciliation might therefore become less difficult if it were offered to the modern world straightforwardly as a principle upon which behaviour should be based. The biblical emphasis could then be placed upon the inspirational example of the life of Jesus, rather than upon formal doctrines built upon his crucifixion.

With the inclusion of the principle of reconciliation, the framework of commitment in modern secular spirituality approaches completion. To use covering titles, the commitments are those of truth, freedom, caring and reconciliation. Summarizing the previous argument, whilst the upholding of freedom requires obedience to the moral law, it is in the nature of caring that it cannot be commanded but must be freely given. Truth and reconciliation are likewise to be freely grasped. Remarkably, for some people those four interwoven commitments seem sufficient in themselves to form the entirety of spiritual life, and they appear to proceed in the total absence of religious belief. Such people, often found working in charitable organizations, inspire wonder at their devotion, given that they enter no apparent hope of any life beyond this present one, or countenance any divine account of this world. But remarkable as such people are, and humbling though their behaviour is, it is doubtful whether they form more than a small minority in the land. A leading figure in the Church of England remarked recently that he thought this country to be largely atheistic in its outlook. Whilst it is an understandable conclusion from within the body of the Church, it may nevertheless be making too much of the evidence of empty pews. Although many people are unable to accept any longer the traditional framework of Christian belief, that does not necessarily restrict them to atheism or even agnosticism. The dual beliefs in God the Creator and in life beyond death continue to be held by many people, albeit the beliefs are often tempered by doubt to the extent of being nearer to hesitant hopes than confident convictions. With regard to the causes of doubt, they are many and diverse, but the presence of evil looms large among them. The need for reconciliation may be recognized and implemented, but that does not of itself resolve the doubts concerning belief in a loving God.

To summarize, modern secular spirituality is broadly characterized by the commitments to truth, freedom, caring and reconciliation, the whole expressed in an environment of belief in God the Creator and in eternal life. But the beliefs are often less than confident and doubts are much in evidence. The commitments themselves are not easy and have to be worked out in the context of tribalism, competition, and the need for esteem. That is the point where the argument has reached, but it must be remarked that it still only provides a framework for spirituality. There remain critical questions concerning the practical ways in which spiritual life can be pursued in political and social affairs, in professional life, and among friends and family. If secular spirituality is to live up to its title, it must engage significantly in all these areas. Issues also remain concerning organized religion, issues around which the argument has merely circled, whilst focusing on the secular. These are matters that will be addressed in the next two chapters. Finally, there remains the question of human destiny, the end to which our spiritual lives, whether secular or religious, are gradually taking us. It is the question that forms the subject matter of the concluding chapter.

This chapter itself still has some unfinished business. Of the importance of reconciliation there is no doubt, even if doctrinal arguments about atonement remain in an unsatisfactory state. But the principal ongoing problem lies in the question of theistic belief, to which only a hesitant answer was given. As the question was put before: if God is omnipotent and good, how did evil arise? The optimistic argument from the moral freedom of individual human beings (spiritual beings) has taken us some of the way, but it is not a complete answer. Freedom is never absolute, and it remains to be shown why the opportunities for human evil should take the particular forms that they do. The commitment to reconciliation helps, but the sheer extent of human suffering still leaves the answer in doubt. Finally, there is the problem of the natural order, as previously raised in Chapter 6. Expressed in fairly basic terms, how is God to be reconciled to the animal that is killed and eaten by the tiger? Is the animal too lowly to need reconciliation? Are its sufferings irrelevant to God? Contrary to appearances, does the animal not actually suffer? Some would argue that animals are not sentient beings, and not therefore able to suffer either pain or fear. As previously remarked, this solution will not satisfy everyone. Of all the doubts, these can be among the sharpest and they may remain unresolved during life on this earth. But spiritual life is complex, and no single set of doubts is necessarily destructive of theistic belief.

Returning to the principal thrust of the argument, given the presence of evil in so much of human life it is evident that reconciliation must be accepted as an essential part of an authentic secular spirituality. For the theist, the processes of repentance and forgiveness that lead to reconciliation will belong both to relations between different human beings and also to those between human beings and God. Broadening the argument, the commitments of secular spirituality have been identified as those of truth, freedom, caring and reconciliation. Beyond the commitments come the issues of belief. As previously remarked, there is a tendency for beliefs in God and eternal life to be held in concert, or denied in concert. Given the need for reconciliation, this tendency is likely to become even stronger. For those who have taken the leap of faith, belief in God is united with trust in his providence. Others, with equal determination, have set aside any such hope or belief. But there are those in the middle, a great many persons as far as can be judged, who hope more than they believe, and who have doubts that may remain with them for the duration of life on this earth. Their hopes are both in God and in the opportunity for life beyond this mortal coil. For this group, one further point can be offered that may be of significance. In Chapter 1, it was shown that human life belonged distinctly to both physical and mental realms. The commitments of secular spirituality, summarized as the commitments to truth, freedom, caring and reconciliation, are all located in the mental realm, even though they issue forth and are given expression in physical action. As such, they constitute just those characteristics of life that can rationally be expected to continue beyond physical death. Although there can be no certainties, there are nevertheless reasonable grounds for supposing that they provide pointers toward ultimate human destiny and the nature of eternity.

Notes

1. Jonathan Clatworthy, *Good God*, Jon Carpenter Publishing, 1997.
2. Revelation 14, esp. vv. 9–11.
3. John A. T. Robinson, *Honest to God*, SCM Press, 1963, and *The New Reformation*, SCM Press, 1965.

8

Life on Earth

The Individual in Society

Four principal commitments characterize modern secular spirituality. Using covering titles, they are the commitments to truth, freedom, caring and reconciliation. Focusing on the state of affairs in this country, whilst caring and reconciliation have been nurtured in a long and deeply rooted Christian tradition, the spiritual commitments to truth and freedom have been the subject of separate and more recent secular development. In modern secular society, opportunities to apply these commitments can arise in many different fields. Particularly prominent among them are those of politics, working life, leisure, the environment and the family.

In connection with these various fields of activity, this chapter has two objectives. The first is to identify some of the principal issues of our time, and the second is to examine their likely impact upon individuals and their spiritual endeavours. The choice of issues is limited and personal. No doubt others would choose very differently. Whatever the particular issue under consideration, however, the intention is to emphasize the relevance to spiritual development. Before reaching the issues themselves, however, some preliminary remarks need to be offered concerning the range of different positions from which individuals can approach the spirituality of their earthly lives.

If life in this world is the only life that we are going to have, then philosophically speaking we can choose between the extremes of enjoying it as much as possible or putting up with it as far as possible. Neither of these positions need preclude us from loving our neighbours, or less extravagantly upholding their human rights, but long-term outcomes will be few in number because of the constraint to a single earthly life. The first position is set out by Edward Fitzgerald in his elegant translation of the Rubaiyat of Omar Khyyam. He declares that we should unashamedly enjoy the brief moment that we have by focusing attention upon those activities that give us immediate pleasure.[1] At the other extreme, vividly portrayed in the novels of Thomas Hardy for example, we should recognize the bleak uncaring nature of reality, and set up such brave and temporary defences as we are able, finding a brief warmth in our lives through the loving agency of family and friends. [2] Between these extremes, it is rationally open to all those who are convinced that this is the only life that they will know to set themselves the goals of wealth or power, or to seek personal status through some particular achievement or rank.

That some people, convinced of these limitations, nevertheless develop a strong spiritual component in their lives - spiritual in the secular sense of the term, certainly not religious - must be a matter of admiration or of wonder. And, as remarked in Chapter 7, it happens. Humanists, for example, join human rights organizations, and work strenuously and selflessly for the temporal freedom and security of their fellow human beings. It seems that no single group of persons possesses a monopoly over the search for truth, the commitment to freedom and human rights, or the exercise of caring and compassion, and persons with an entirely this-worldly philosophy are to be found wholeheartedly dedicated to such causes.

For many people, however, almost certainly a majority in Britain, the philosophic position is much less precise. Uncertainties about immortality, doubts about the presence of God, although apparently constituting the mental states of the majority seem only rarely to develop into outright disbelief. Whilst the earlier signs of religious belief may be missing, the wistful hope maintains that the spiritual journey may not reach its final conclusion as 'dust returns to dust'.

So spiritual life continues in secular form upon earth, certainly in the British part of it upon which this text is chiefly focused, although often in a mood of hope rather than belief. It is important, however, to recognize just how many and great are the problems. The absence of traditional religious doctrine ensures a difficult start, and subsequently hazards and obstacles beset the spiritual journey. The thrusts of physical and economic needs and desires are powerful, and it does not help to assume that they can be straightforwardly opposed as if they were unequivocally evil. The Christian baptism service of old included a prayer for Christians to be victorious over 'the devil, the world, and the flesh'. Nowadays, most people are 'world-affirming' and would no longer be prepared to lump 'the world, and the flesh' with the devil. Nor in many cases would they even believe in the devil. Similar kinds of arguments apply to the pressures of tribalism and competition, which can lead to terrible wrongs, but cannot simply be dismissed as wrong in themselves. Finally, it is almost inevitable that modern spiritual life will become subject to the desire for esteem, the powerful and near universal desire for a sense of self-worth.

It seems, therefore, that those who enter into the commitments of secular spirituality will find that life on earth confronts them with a host of problems. Exploring ways in which the problems can be worked out, this argument must inevitably be selective. There are simply too many people engaged in too many separate activities for it to be sensible to do more than choose a handful of issues. It is hoped nevertheless to give some expression to the common spiritual themes, irrespective of the particular activity. As previously indicated, the issues to be explored are located in politics, working life, leisure, the environment and the family.

Political Extremes

The twentieth century witnessed first the upsurge and then the defeat of the two political extremes of fascism and communism. At the beginning of the twenty-first century, it is just a little too easy to assume that these successive defeats were inevitable, and that, in consequence, the underlying philosophies of their movements can now safely be ignored. Being born at almost the same time that Hitler came to power in Germany, and having lived much of my life first in World War Two and then in the Cold War, I am acutely aware of how terribly easily things could have been different. Perhaps fascism and communism alike have gone forever as significant political creeds, but it would not be wise to base the hope of future generations upon the facile confidence that it must be so.

In brief, fascism carries tribalism to an extreme and points it in the direction of the nation state. An individual obtains his or her value as a human being only by becoming a loyal citizen of the state. In return for the value and esteem thus conferred, the individual owes an absolute duty of (military) service to the nation. Nations strive against one another in war, and the defeated nations are held in servitude by their conquerors. Quite literally, citizens of defeated states are liable to be taken as slaves by their victors. Fascism takes the evolutionary idea of 'survival of the fittest' and extends it to the 'triumph of the fittest'. The less fit may actually survive, but only in servitude.

The brevity of this account testifies to its being drastically simplified, but it nevertheless conveys enough of the essential nature of fascism to meet present purposes. Fascism carries a simple, powerful and direct appeal to the human sense of tribalism, as expressed in patriotism. It appeals similarly and intensely to the sense of competition. It addresses the human need for esteem by conferring it through citizenship of the nation. By responding in this near-absolute way to tribalism, competition and esteem, fascism leaves no place in the conduct of its affairs for truth, freedom, caring and reconciliation. They may continue to apply among family members and neighbours, but only providing that they do not hinder the progress of the nation state in the struggle with its competitors.

Communism constitutes both an economic and a political philosophy. It is sometimes argued that if the economics could be separated from the oppressive politics, it could provide a viable alternative to free markets and capitalism. Karl Marx stated the underlying principle:

'From each according to his abilities, to each according to his needs.' [3]

Moral arguments continue for and against the basic economic theory. Communism's most terrible features arise, however, from the political methods that are used to persuade people to accept the principle. To achieve its purpose, communism defines a tribalism of the working class, and an intensely competitive tribalism at that. Within the working class, the outcomes are supposedly beneficial and egalitarian. In order to impose the system upon society, however, the working class has to set up a political dictatorship – a dictatorship of the proletariat. Tragically, this form of dictatorship can be as oppressive as any known in human history. In theory, the outcomes of communism should be less dreadful than those of fascism. In practice, there seems remarkably little to choose between them.

Spiritual life cannot be destroyed either by fascism or communism. Brave souls will still find a way. But the grim reality is that neither the commitment to truth nor to human rights can do much more than struggle for survival in a fascist or communist dictatorial environment. Basically, the first two elements of secular spirituality are liable to institutional extinction. Happily, neither of these extreme political creeds has retained serious credibility as the world enters the twenty-first century, but it would be unwise to assume that there could be no resurgence. For the present, however, liberal democracy has become the prevailing political philosophy, challenged only by extreme forms of Islamic theocratic beliefs. This does not mean that liberal democracy is universal, however, as there are still parts of the world in which military dictators or local warlords occupy positions of power. In China, communism as a political creed has lost its authority, but democracy shows little sign of taking its place. What these non-democratic states lack, however, is any form of philosophic political grounding for their present forms of government. Excepting the few applications of Islamic religion to the governance of the nation state, liberal democracy today provides the framework for political thought.

Warfare

Given the dominance of democracy, the good news is that liberal democracies are unlikely to go to war with one another. At least, that is what the history of liberal democracies tells us. The brief conflicts between India and Pakistan over Kashmir, and the war between Britain and the United States that occurred two centuries ago in 1812, are the only major instances. (Those with a mind for tidy solutions argue that the latter did not really count as a conflict between democracies, as Britain did not meet even the most limited criteria for liberal democracy until after the first reform bill of 1832.) Those conflicts excepted, there seem to have been no examples at all in recent history of democracies warring with one another. Unhappily though, when liberal democracy was absent, if only on one side, warfare in the last century was terrible and frequent. The harsh truth is that democracy and freedom were only sustained because the populations of the principal democratic states were willing to fight ferociously in their defence. Times have clearly changed, but it would still be a very optimistic person who would feel confident that liberal democracy will never again be in need of military defence. Furthermore, although the risk of a global war has diminished, the probability and actuality of smaller conflicts remain. As such, the spiritual implications of armed conflict remain highly relevant to the exploration of life on earth.

Whilst the causes that individuals adopt when they go to war may be those of freedom and democracy, straightforward tribalism in national patriotic form is what often predominates. No doubt there are many different reasons that prompt individuals to volunteer for military service, or to accept the draft, but commitment to country is almost certainly to be found toward the head of the list. The spiritual significance of such a point needs to be emphasized. For most ordinary people, there are not many causes for which they would agree to kill or risk being killed. Tribalism, expressed in the form of patriotic commitment to the nation state, is one of the few. In exploring spiritual issues, it is vital not to underestimate the significance of tribalism. Going to war may or may not be the right thing to do, but it cannot be disconnected from individual spiritual life, and neither therefore can the tribalism that so often constitutes the impetus for military action.

The moral issues raised by warfare are both complex and acute. Article 3 of the Universal Declaration of Human Rights (UDHR) asserts that everyone has the right to life, liberty and security of person. Some people, either on the basis of that article or upon a similar argument, conclude that a human life should never be deliberately taken, and therefore become pacifists. Others interpret the article more flexibly to mean that a life can only be deliberately taken in the immediate defence of one's own life or that of another human being. Such an interpretation allows, for example, the occasional use of firearms by the police. It is the interpretation that most people and seemingly all governments put upon the declaration.

But the problem with warfare is that it goes much further than that. Soldiers in time of war are not constrained to killing one another only in immediate self-defence or in the defence of others. On the contrary, they can engage in offensive actions, seeking out and killing their opponents, without needing any defensive justification. In time of war or armed conflict, therefore, soldiers (the term 'soldier' is used in a generic sense) in large measure give up that most elemental of human rights, the right to 'life, liberty and security of person'. In its place they acquire the right to kill. This marks a fundamental departure from the UDHR, but it is rarely recognized as such. Governments, Churches, human rights organizations – none of them is at all keen to grasp this particular nettle. No simple answer is available in this text. Pacifism is not a route that many people will follow. In its absence, a fundamental reappraisal is needed of the nature of human rights in a time of armed conflict.

Moving on to the practice of war, if the right to kill is not to be indiscriminate, some framework of law will be required. That is not easy. Indeed, according to Cicero: 'Laws are silent in time of war.'[4] There may be more force to Cicero's statement than is commonly recognized, a point to be returned to later. The current position in international law, however, is that the rules defined in 1949 by the four Geneva Conventions[5] are widely accepted as forming the humanitarian basis for the conduct of war. In fact, there is a further substantial body of international protocols and conventions relating to the conduct of war, some preceding and some succeeding the 1949 Conventions, but it is those four conventions that are most commonly regarded as forming the international legal basis for the conduct of armed conflict. In a rough and ready sense, therefore, the UDHR is set aside in time of war, at least as far as soldiers are concerned, and the rules of the Geneva Conventions take over in its place.

The process seems straightforward, but there are in fact the most acute problems. The moment of transfer from UHDR to Geneva Convention is clearly critical. The action of soldiers seeking out and killing one another in offensive engagements is only legitimized after the transfer has occurred. The moment is defined by the commencement of a war or armed conflict. But what determines the commencement? In essence, the action of the soldiers in seeking out and killing one another in offensive engagements! There may be some written declaration, but that is not essential. There is therefore a sense in which wars and armed conflicts are self-defining, and the fundamental shift in the framework of law occurs through a kind of circular process within which the great majority of people, whether soldiers or otherwise, have no effective say. The right to life for soldiers is set aside simply because some people have decided to set it aside!

The next problem is the distinction between soldier and civilian. The Geneva Conventions are built upon the notion of warfare as something in which only soldiers participate, with the civilian population watching from the sidelines and trying not to get hit by stray bullets (or whatever is being fired). This works reasonably well for strictly limited conflicts, like the Falklands war for example. Tragically, in that conflict one stray British shell killed three civilian women sheltering in a house, but, with that exception, the armed forces fought their battles in isolation and the civilian population was able to keep out of the way. When a war becomes total, however, as in World War Two for example, the rules for the 'model' conflict soon prove inadequate. According to the rules, the husband who is conscripted, put in uniform and sent to the front, can be killed legitimately in half a hundred different ways. His wife, who lives at home and works in a munitions factory, remains a civilian and cannot legitimately be attacked. She makes the shells, he fires them. She is inviolate (in theory); he can be attacked at any time (unless he is in hospital injured). In a total war, when the production of shells is no less vital than their use, this distinction is simply not going to be maintained. Furthermore, in World War Two there was a strongly held belief in

Britain that the nation was fighting a 'people's war', a war in which the whole community was involved. On that basis the British accepted the bombing of their own cities and then replied with terrible strength. In so far as the bombing was contrary to the laws of war, it follows that a large part of the British adult population could have been indicted for war crimes! Evidence tends to be anecdotal, but it does seem that it was not just a few 'wicked' leaders but virtually the whole community that supported the bomber offensive against Germany. People did so believing that the onslaught formed a necessary part of bringing about the defeat of Nazism. No bomber offensive, no apparent departure from the laws of war, and the gas chambers of Auschwitz might be working to this day! This is a horrible issue, but mere adherence to the letter of international law will not be sufficient to produce a commonly acceptable moral solution. Where the distinction between soldiers and civilians is concerned, the present basis of international law is profoundly unsatisfactory, and needs urgent and fundamental review.

(To be technically correct, the Geneva Conventions, to which reference has been made, were not adopted until after World War Two, so they could not apply other than retrospectively to that conflict. The Geneva Conventions were based upon earlier laws, however, including the Hague Convention that pre-dates World War One. An extrapolation of these earlier laws, from land warfare to aerial warfare and bombing, led to the legal and moral claims that have been levelled against the strategic bomber offensive. Almost certainly, however, any change that might be introduced nowadays would be related to the 1949 Conventions or their subsequent protocols.)

The penultimate problem with human rights and the Geneva Conventions relates once again to the distinctions between war and peace, and soldiers and civilians. It is exemplified in all its discomfort by the recent conflict in Northern Ireland. The British Government never accepted that a war or armed conflict was taking place, and, in consequence, British soldiers were severely constrained in the circumstances in which they were permitted to open fire. To all intents and purposes, they had to behave as if they were armed police dealing with armed criminals, not soldiers engaging members of an opposing army. Yet this insistence upon the absence of war was succeeded by protracted negotiations 'in search of peace', and frequent references to organizations participating in 'the ceasefire'. Sadly for the soldiers, however, even the presence of these negotiations did not lead to any official recognition that they had been participating in a conflict. This kind of ambiguity over the role of the armed forces, of which Northern Ireland is but one example, operates almost always to the disadvantage of professional servicemen. Once again, the present framework of both national and international law is unsatisfactory.

The final difficulty concerns the documents themselves. The notion that the UDHR gives way to the Geneva Conventions in time of war is undoubtedly convenient and is also conceptually tidy - until one compares the actual documents. At that point the exercise looks less convincing, because they are simply not two of a kind. The UDHR is strong on general principle, but contains few details and virtually no practice. In contrast, the Geneva Conventions are weak on issues of principle, but focus strongly on practical detail. The documents are not natural alternatives. Furthermore, the Geneva Conventions say nothing about the purposes of war, but are based nevertheless on the underlying assumption that they cannot include genocide. Therein lies an immediate limitation. People facing a foe intent on genocide will do what they believe they have to do in order to protect themselves, irrespective of the regulations of the Geneva Conventions. In that respect, the conventions tend to lose touch with common perceptions of morality. This exemplifies a more general problem, which is the distinction between the actual conduct of war, *jus in bello*, and the right of resort to war, *jus ad bellum*. Formally these are held in separation, but both in reality and in morality they will often need to be brought together. When this happens, question marks are liable be put against the relevance of *jus in bello,* and Cicero's dictum of laws being silent in time of war will need to be remembered.

In view of this list of comments, it might seem that the whole value of the Geneva Conventions is being questioned. That is not correct. Particularly in limited conflicts, the conventions play a vital part in keeping the dreadful nature of war within some kind of boundary. Furthermore, when the conflict is over, nations and peoples that have endeavoured to keep within the conventions stand a much better chance of achieving a form of reconciliation. At least they start from the common ground of having behaved properly towards their respective prisoners of war, and of having made some effort to spare civilians from the battle. What is urgently required for the Geneva Conventions is amendment, not rejection.

Where does all this leave the individual and his or her spiritual concerns? The relationship between the UDHR and the Geneva Conventions is at present both unclear and ill-considered. There is an almost casual assumption that when a person dons a military uniform, he or she abandons the right to 'life, liberty and security of person'. The Geneva Conventions themselves are both limited and flawed. In particular, there is no attempt to define the role of the quasi-combatant, the civilian who becomes actively, if indirectly, involved in the prosecution of war. These are matters that need urgent yet thoughtful re-examination by governments, by religious bodies, and also by other non-governmental agencies such as the Red Cross and human rights organizations. Indeed, these are also matters for individual citizens, whose lives can be so dramatically influenced by the onset of armed conflict. Clearly the events of 11 September 2001 and the subsequent 'war against terror' have given an additional emphasis and urgency to all these issues. These are not matters that are ordinarily regarded as spiritual, but in the context of modern secular spirituality, that is how they need to be approached.

One hopeful sign in this country is the growth of human rights education in schools, a development encouraged by the pioneering work of Amnesty International. Many school children today are aware of the UDHR and recognize its importance. But the further step to consider the Geneva Conventions and their relationships with the UDHR is not something that is yet happening. There is a need to press for such an agenda. A greater understanding of the problems of relating human rights to humanitarian law is something that would benefit the whole of society. None of us can safely ignore the issues of war and peace, and they belong in the midst of secular spirituality.

Liberal Democracy, Free Markets and Capitalism

With the Cold War more than a decade concluded, one of the most important political issues today for the people of Europe, including the United Kingdom, is the development of the European Union. Few in Europe today would argue about the need to maintain democracy, freedom and human rights, and to endeavour to do so in a peaceful environment. Uncomfortably, however, that was not an achievement that Europe had shown itself to be capable of delivering by its own efforts during the last century. Left to itself, it is virtually certain that continental Europe would have remained under fascist control in the years following Hitler's early successes in the 1940s. Even with that threat overcome, much of the continent would almost certainly have succumbed to communism in the second half of the century, had it not been for the protection of the American shield in NATO. Nowadays no such immediate threats to freedom and human rights exist, yet proponents of the European Union often argue that one of its principal functions is to prevent the recurrence of such dangers.

One does not have to doubt their sincerity in order to have serious misgivings about their wisdom. The European Union is beloved of many politicians, but not of many citizens. It is weak in democratic accountability, with its institutions suffering from what is aptly described as a 'democratic deficit'. Furthermore, it has been an evident prey to corruption. In a continent whose people have shown such a limited internal capacity to sustain freedom and human rights, this thrust toward a closer political union carries with it many dangers. At worst, the absence of strong democratic structures could lead to a resurgence of the very kind of tyranny that the Union supposedly exists to withstand. Furthermore, the lack of enthusiasm for a supra-national state is already making itself known in the revival of extreme right wing political bodies at the national level, and any attempt to combat such bodies through the agency of the Union itself would carry its own risk of escalation.

There are reasons enough to question whether the whole enterprise is flawed. To prevent any repetition of the horrors of the first half of the twentieth century, the requirement in Europe is for a dedicated effort within the individual nation states to uphold personal freedom and minority rights, and to build strongly democratic systems. It is unhelpful and possibly even dangerous to focus attention instead upon the development of a (federal) international body that is seriously lacking in democracy at the supra-national level. In addition, there must be concerns about any further strengthening of an operating commission whose actions already seem to have stretched far beyond the control or even the influence of ordinary citizens. There may be good reasons for the further development of a European economic community, but the attempt to move toward a still closer political union is an altogether more questionable project.

Turning from the international future of the European Union to the internal affairs of individual nations, the principal mode of government in the Western world has become that of liberal democracy. With its rise, however, has come a near totality of capitalism and free markets. There is no absolute reason why liberal democracy should be so closely accompanied by this form of economic system. Nationalization is not incompatible with democracy, nor is there any overriding democratic objection to the determination by Government of prices and incomes. In practice, however, this is not what is happening. Furthermore, such is the strength of the combined thrust toward democracy, private investment and the competitive negotiation of prices and wages that it can even be described without impossible exaggeration as constituting the end of history. Francis Fukuyama, who advances that argument, makes it clear that it does not mean the end of history in the sense that the world will witness no more events, but rather that the human race has now reached an effective consensus on matters of politics and economics. Whereas previously different political and economic theories struggled for supremacy, now there is only one set of ideas holding a position of dominance. Unless that situation changes, Fukuyama argues that the history of human political and economic development has reached its conclusion. [6]

Two quite different issues follow. The first is the question whether this seemingly irresistible thrust towards democracy, free markets and capitalism is fully international. In *The Mystery of Capital*, Hernando de Soto argues that, although the concepts of free markets and capitalism have been vigorously exported from the West to the countries of the developing world, the process so far has been conspicuous by its failure.[7] Capitalism is triumphant in the West but in many Third World countries and one-time Communist states it is not triumphing at all. A solution is offered by de Soto, a thoughtful one that does not involve a departure from capitalism, but instead its deliberate extension to the poorer people of the developing world by the registration of their land

and property. But however significant Hernando de Soto's solution may be in itself, it does not seem to be complete. On the evidence of the West and the arguments for secular spirituality, commitments at a national level to human rights and education will also be essential if the living standards of the poorest people are to be significantly raised and the quality of their lives enriched. Furthermore, aid from the Western world to provide help in situations of famine will probably be needed for many years to come. In the interim, claims for the 'end of history' may have to be put on hold!

The second point concerns life in the capitalist western world. Liberal democracy allied to free markets and capitalism provides a structural basis for the upholding of freedom and human rights and a sufficient capacity to meet the majority of human physical needs. It also provides a suitable amphitheatre for competition and the quest for esteem. But that is not the whole of the story. An aspect of free markets and capitalism that is frequently in evidence is the relentless search for wealth. To a certain degree, efforts to acquire substantial wealth can be of value, both to the persons who are thus engaged and to society as a whole. Entrepreneurs - whether corporate businessmen or individual practitioners - encourage the growth of the Gross National Product and thereby increase the provision of goods and services available to the whole community. And certainly, a great many people need to have jobs - and the money that goes with them - in order to provide a decent standard of living for themselves and their dependents. But there is a darker side. The rush to acquire money all too easily leaves the weakest and most vulnerable of society in material discomfort and without a sense of status. Furthermore, the acquisition of money only provides the holders with the tokens for goods and services to be taken from society - it may or may not be an accurate measure of how much they have put in!

This ushers the argument into those vast and important fields of social and political activity, extending beyond human rights and touching upon both personal and social morality. In particular, it leads to the kind of arguments for and against major social change - including the broad redistribution of wealth - that belonged to British socialism in the early years after World War Two. The arguments are well known. They are strongly egalitarian and include commitments to the material well-being of the whole community. The approach is wholly democratic and includes the commitments to freedom and human rights. In terms of British political history, they were the ideas that came to fruition under the Labour Governments of Prime Ministers Attlee, Wilson and Callaghan. They led to the widespread nationalization of industry, and to the development of the welfare state. In the 1980s, however, the British people turned away collectively from such policies. They did so, it seemed, in the belief that trade unions had become too powerful, working practices too restrictive, and productivity too low. In consequence, during the last two decades of the twentieth century, private enterprise, free markets and capitalism became the widely accepted basis for economic life. Furthermore, that development came to apply not only in the United Kingdom but also in virtually all the countries of the western world.

Notwithstanding the current strength of private enterprise and capitalism, it is not beyond possibility that a form of democratic socialism, akin to that attempted in this country in the years immediately after World War Two, might be tried again in more benign circumstances and to beneficial effect. On the other hand, it is important not to underestimate either the failings of socialism in the 1970s, or the benefits that flowed from the economic changes of the 1980s. On balance, it seems improbable that anything very different from the present system of free markets and capitalism will hold sway in this country for the next decade or more. These remarks are therefore constrained to operate on the assumption that liberal democracy, free markets and capitalism will continue to characterize the political scene in the United Kingdom during the foreseeable years.

From a spiritual standpoint, the combination of liberal democracy, free markets and capitalism would seem to have a good chance of providing a society within which freedom and human rights are sustained, and competition and the desire for esteem satisfied, at least for the majority. Furthermore, given an education system not greatly dissimilar from that which presently obtains, the pursuit of truth should continue to be effectively nurtured. But what of caring and compassion? How are they to be related to society and its politics? Welfare provision via taxation provides part of the answer, and, notwithstanding the cut and thrust of party politics, there is a substantial measure of agreement in the United Kingdom about the kind of provision that is needed. Taxation also plays a part in establishing minimum standards of living, grappling with unemployment and defeating the 'poverty trap'. Beyond that, taxation is also reasonably assumed to be required as part of the national response to poverty overseas. The last is a whole subject in itself, but the magnitude of an appropriate response is beyond the immediate scope of this argument.

Beyond those identified elements, however, it is questionable whether it is spiritually appropriate to make deliberate use of taxation as a means of redistributing wealth within the bounds of a single nation. In this context, health, education, and welfare provision are not regarded as forming part of such a redistribution. They have their own separate rationale. Such important aspects apart, however, there is a substantial argument that individual human beings - spiritual beings - need to be as free as possible to exercise their own judgement, enterprise and morality, both in acquiring money and in deciding how to use it. It remains for religious organizations to remind their members (and non-members if they choose to listen) that 'you cannot take it with you'.

They can also press the argument that charity is important and that spiritual development is hindered rather than helped by an undue attachment to material wealth. Of course, this does not solve the question of the lack of status that may be associated with a lack of wealth. Perhaps there is no answer that is likely to be universally accepted, but the following points can be emphasized:

(a) Activities have a value although they do not always have a price, e.g. activities that belong to the family, or that are charitable, social or religious in nature.

(b) Wealth has only a limited function (beyond the level needed to escape from poverty) in providing happiness. Moreover, the dignity and value of every human being is established irrespective of his/her income and material possessions. Wealth is a measure of what an individual can take from society, not what he/she puts in!

(c) The nature of spiritual goals are not limited to the confines of 'this mortal coil', but extend beyond the inevitable loss of 'treasures on earth' when life in this world is ended.

The issue of power is similar but subtler. Clearly the desire for power is felt very strongly by some people. It is not enough, however, simply to dismiss it as evil. 'Power corrupts and absolute power corrupts absolutely'. Let us hope not! Power certainly can corrupt, but it does not have to. It can be used responsibly, decently, and can benefit both those who exercise it and those over whom it is exercised. The desire for power and the use of power are not simply to be identified as evil. It is necessary to look to the manner in which power is sought and applied - evil may surface in either but its presence should not be presumed.

Although it is not appropriate to dismiss wealth, power and the concomitant desire for status as intrinsically evil, their capacity to generate evil must be taken with the utmost seriousness. The spiritual journey is not necessarily in the direction of uplifting and morally pure goals. To the doubts that are for so many the inevitable accompaniments of the spiritual life, there have to be added the pressures of the earthly desires for wealth and power, desires that are all the more confusing for being ambiguous in their morality. All too easily, amid the confusion, high sounding words about the spiritual nature of caring, compassion and charity acquire a hollow ring. Life on earth is difficult, and the absence of clear spiritual signposts adds to the difficulties. Nevertheless, for a secular spirituality to be consistent with previous arguments it must include the political will to use taxation for the implementation of a welfare programme, to establish minimum standards of living, and to contribute to the overcoming of poverty overseas.

Work and Leisure

During my working life in higher education, there were number of occasions when I heard lecturing staff talk of the time when students would complete their studies and enter 'the real world'. By 'the real world' they meant the world of paid employment, the world of professional work. If the choice of words was a little problematic, the fundamental importance the speakers attached to the forthcoming professional activity was entirely clear. Recognizing the importance of work, however, is not the same as becoming idealistic about it. The reality of paid employment is that it is first and foremost about earning a living. Our hunter-gatherer predecessors did not hunter-gather for the good of their souls, they hunter-gathered to provide for their bodies, and if they failed they starved. Today, those in Britain who do not work are unlikely to starve, but their lives are still going to be fairly uncomfortable. For many people, in practice there is little choice but to work long hours in order to pay water rates, gas and electricity bills, and to handle the grocery checkout account. Jobs may or may not be otherwise worthwhile or enjoyable, but they do have to be undertaken in order to meet life's essential or near essential material needs.

'The real world' is also the place in which people deploy their talents, physical or mental. For many, this too is an essential aspect of work - life is incomplete and profoundly so if talents are underused or allowed to atrophy. In certain cases, this aspect of work becomes a spiritual activity. The spiritual embraces the higher faculties, and creative talents come within their span. Once again, however, it is important not to become idealistic about it. The use of faculties may extend beyond the strictly utilitarian to include a spiritual component, but that is by no means always the case, and it does not help to imagine that it is.

This is part of a more general point, which is that life itself is not wholly spiritual, and that mental beings are liable to become unbalanced if they think or behave as if it were. There are in fact two quite different ways in which the spiritual can be over-emphasized. The first arises through the deliberate attempt to minimize or subdue the non-spiritual aspects of life. This is the kind of endeavour illustrated by the astringent excess of Dryden's Good Parson, who:

'Refined himself to soul, to curb the sense
And made almost a sin of abstinence.' [8]

A self-imposed ordinance of world denial carries with it the danger of a complete loss of ordinary good sense! The other and opposite risk is that of assuming that virtually the whole of life is in some way spiritual, or ought to be, in which case almost anything that is done in 'the real world' becomes by necessity a matter for the soul. For a properly balanced life, both of these extremes need to be avoided, and that applies as much in 'the real world' as anywhere else.

These cautionary comments being duly entered, it is time to progress to the higher faculty of *thymos* and remark that the world of professional working life can engage it in a number of ways. Assuming that *thymos* in the work place is not going to be fundamentally different from *thymos* anywhere else, it must be expected that a significant proportion of the *thymotic* content of professional life would be derived from the tribal and competitive elements of human nature, and the near universal desire for esteem. For any one individual, the situation will often be complex, with intellect, talent, conscience and 'heart' all involved and interwoven with natural desire and physical need.

Tribalism is particularly dominant in uniformed services - the military, police, fire service, nursing service and so on. It leads to people working closely together and caring for one another, which is as it should be, but sadly it can also lead to dismissive or disparaging behaviour toward others who belong outside the service. Tribalism tends to count for rather less in other occupations, but the desire to compete is often very strong. Indeed the very basis of free markets is competition. Once again this can be healthy, providing that competition is kept within properly understood and commonly accepted bounds, but sadly this is not always the case. One way of climbing the ladder of professional success is to tread heavily on the fingers of those a little lower down! Competition figures prominently within companies or other professional organizations, particularly those with large numbers of employees. People struggle for positions of seniority, and it is not always clear which methods of competition are acceptable and which are not. There is a basic dilemma here. Loving a professional neighbour may not seem consistent with intense efforts to secure promotion over his or her head. So what happens? Does a commitment to spiritual values entail remaining at the bottom of the promotional ladder?

The issue of promotion or career progression is not narrowly one of competition. The associated question of esteem also figures prominently, as does the desire for greater wealth. *Thymotic* desires can extend to a professional megalomania, the desire to be seen as superior in some way to other employees. Greater wealth may be desired straightforwardly, because a person wants to buy a bigger house, a faster car, a newer yacht, or unselfishly wishes to provide material support for other members of the family. Alternatively, more wealth may be desired for less happy *thymotic* reasons, in order not merely to 'keep up with the Joneses', but to get ahead of them. How in all this does one discover what is the spiritually correct thing to do? To repeat an already heavily used response - there is no simple answer! Naive talk about caring and compassion, and the dismissal of anything else as sin, just invites people to assume that the spiritual and the professional simply cannot be put together.

The beginning of an answer lies in the recognition that, if freedom and human rights are thought to belong to one side of a coin, then justice and fair play will be found on the other. In seeking to advance a career and simultaneously to uphold the spiritual dimension of life, a person must endeavour to eschew any actions that are contrary to justice and fair play. By including the reference to fair play, there is clearly a shift beyond the bare framework of freedom and human rights as previously defined, an extension of the argument in order to encompass more fully the professional aspects of life. If justice is regarded as the formal process whereby freedom and human rights are upheld, then fair play is the informal extension of that idea to the constraint of actions in the working place (among others), so that human decency as well as human rights shall obtain.

What needs to be recognized is that neither justice nor fair play requires a denial of competition, or entails the abandonment of the struggle for esteem. What they are able to do is provide the ground rules for the working place, within which the struggles for promotion, money and esteem, can properly be undertaken. 'Fair play' has been used as a covering title. In some organizations, what is regarded as fair play may be developed into a code of conduct, with disciplinary processes and grievance procedures provided in support of the code. To a degree this does formalize the concept (previously described as informal!), but not to the extent that involves courts of law and the full judicial protection of human rights. In any case, from (considerable) personal experience, it does not seem that the wider extension of these quasi-judicial processes works particularly well. Formal rules tend to sit rather uncomfortably between actual law on the one hand, and the wholly informal aspects of fair play on the other. On the whole, it seems preferable that formal internal procedures in support of a moral code should be kept as brief and simple as possible. In other respects, the notions of decency and fair play should be encouraged on an informal basis, so as to illuminate professional behaviour and provide a common moral basis for action. In practice, the arrival of the European Convention on Human Rights will inevitably expand the role of the courts in professional disputes, a tendency that renders even more desirable the concomitant strengthening of the informal practices. With these various markers established, it then belong to individuals in the work place to form their own judgements, and to follow personally chosen spiritual paths in adopting tribal values (which will often be union values), in determining to compete, and in searching for esteem.

What then of those further components of spiritual life, the commitments to caring and compassion? As previously indicated, they will have to be pursued in association with tribalism, competition and the struggle for esteem. Furthermore, they will have to be pursued in situations where the earning of a living - providing for basic material needs - has to take priority. Nothing therefore will be easy, nor will it do simply to dismiss anything that does not advance the cause of caring and compassion as sinful. Providing that human rights are upheld and the informal codes are applied, nothing more can properly be demanded, although that is not to deny that much more may still be hoped.

In all this, secular spirituality faces a danger on two fronts. The first is that individuals, seeking a spiritual dimension to their lives, may conclude that the potential issues of working life are just too complex, that it is better to regard work simply as a means of earning a living, and seek the spiritual aspects of life only in overtly religious activity - worship, prayer, Bible reading, or meditation. The other more serious risk is that persons will assume that the decline in religious belief and practice extends to all forms of spirituality, and conclude that there is no significant spiritual dimension to be found in contemporary life, whether professional or otherwise.

The response to these twin dangers must lie in the vigorous positive advocacy of secular spirituality in the work place, recognizing the difficulties but not surrendering to them. As explained, the insistence on a secular spirituality does not imply the abandonment of religious belief. What it may involve, depending upon the particular beliefs of the individual, is the inclusion of the notion of eternity in what would otherwise be entirely this-earthly temporal considerations. Where that is the case, the spiritual path may not be easy to identify, but it will certainly include 'the real world' of working life on its route.

Work does not consist exclusively of paid employment. In the United Kingdom, voluntary work is also undertaken in a remarkable variety of organizations, many of them formally registered as charities. From the running of football clubs for children to the provision of luncheon clubs for the elderly, the range of activity is vast. The nature of such activity is palpably spiritual. Essentially it belongs within the field of caring – the very heart of spiritual life. It is one of the happier aspects of life in this country, and from a spiritual standpoint needs to be given every encouragement.

Looking beyond working life, whether paid or voluntary, British society has also seen in recent times an expansion of leisure and recreational activity. It is pertinent to ask how far these leisure activities possess a spiritual component. As frequently discussed, spirituality includes both commitments and beliefs. It also includes human creativity, about which comparatively little has yet been said. Previous generations have recognized this form of spiritual activity in such religious examples as the epic poetry of John Milton or the oratorios of George Handel. In the modern world of secular spirituality, the net has to be cast altogether wider. For the more fortunate, the chance to be creative is found within professional employment, but for many others, probably the majority, it is the availability of leisure time that provides the principal opportunity. The breadth of creative activity is vast: from the traditional arts to the creation of gardens, from the construction of model ships to the artistry of ballroom dancing. It should be added that appreciation is often as necessary as the creative act itself. After all, pictures are to be seen, and poems to be read! The role of the appreciative onlooker may not be as great as that of the artist, but it should never be discounted.

Much earlier, in Chapter 1, it was explained that any decision taken in the mental realm and issuing forth in physical action must be either physically creative or destructive. It would be stretching definitions too far, however, to regard all such decisions as having a spiritual element. A more reasonable approach would be to regard sequences of creative decisions, sequences expressive of a person's talents and deriving from them, as belonging collectively within the frame of secular spirituality.

The inclusion of creativity within spirituality is rendered pertinent for theists by the thought that God is Himself the Creator. In the first words of Genesis: 'In the beginning God created the heaven and the earth.'[9]

God is thought of first and foremost as the Creator. Thereafter, different beliefs point in different directions, but creation remains fundamental. For people with theistic beliefs, the exercise of individual talents in creative endeavour is properly seen as being a Godlike activity, and thus belonging inescapably within the realm of spirituality. When spirituality was thought of almost wholly in religious terms, then the forms of creativity that were seen as spiritual were those that pertained to belief and ecclesiastical activity – sacred music for example, and religious paintings and sculptures. But if spirituality can also be secular, the scope widens. Any genuine manifestation of human creative activity can be seen as belonging within the spiritual span, irrespective of whether it has any overt religious connotation. Given the extent of creativity involved in leisure activities, it would seem that leisure may have more of the spiritual about it than might initially seem likely!

Environment

War and peace, democracy and freedom, work and leisure, these are not the only issues that confront society as a whole at the beginning of the third millennium. There is also the environment, and the rights of creatures other than humankind. The widely favoured economic system of capitalism and free trade will not of itself provide for the proper care of the environment, or act to protect the interests of the many other creatures that live on earth with the human race. Can logging companies, for example, in their endeavour to make substantial profits for their shareholders, be expected to have the preservation of forests at the top of their agenda? Preservation will often require actions by governments and judgements by Courts of Law, and these will need to be encouraged by independent organizations such as Greenpeace and

Friends of the Earth. In this respect, it is important to recognize what can reasonably be expected from our economic and trading system. Directors of companies are not being wicked in seeking to satisfy their shareholders by paying substantial dividends. That is what they are employed to do. It is of course necessary for them to keep to the law in the course of their actions. What is required therefore is that the law itself should say the right things and be properly implemented. Care of the environment depends therefore on effective laws and rigorous law enforcement. Happily, in a democracy, it is open to us all to take a share in that process, by supporting pressure groups or by communicating directly with our parliamentary representatives.

In like manner, from recent experience in Britain it does not seem appropriate that the farming community should be the sole determinants of the standards of farming production. Neither should countryside workers be left unchecked to decide how to care decently for the creatures that they rear. The obtaining of high safety standards of food for human beings will have plenty of advocates, even if they are sometimes a little late into action, but the proper treatment of reared animals will need all the efforts that can be mustered by organizations such as Compassion in World Farming. The issue of the protection of wildlife is also important, with the particular problem of hunting very much to the fore.

The question of hunting with dogs has been the subject of active debate in Britain for many years. As people on both sides feel very strongly, the argument tends to become both complex and heated, but there is one particular point concerning the hunting of foxes that does seem undeniable. If a lame fox is unable to run properly and is caught and killed almost at once, there is little satisfaction for the hunters. It is only when the terrified animal is both swift and strong that the hunt is enjoyed. The more prolonged the suffering, the greater the satisfaction. Upon that basis, the case for a ban on hunting is persuasive. Of course the question of the possible erosion of civil liberties is also clearly important. As previously argued, the issue of human rights is central to spiritual concerns, and the need to protect individual liberty is sufficiently great that the law should never lightly be invoked to constrain freedom of action. But the subject of fox hunting is one of calculated cruelty. There is no moral argument to say that civil liberty should extend to the freedom deliberately to inflict cruelty on an animal for the purposes of enjoyment. This last point is clearly of wider application than hunting, but it is certainly strong enough and relevant enough to justify a general ban upon fox hunting, and more widely upon other forms of hunting with dogs.

It is perhaps worth extending this discussion to look at a particular form of defence that is sometimes used by proponents of hunting. This is the argument claiming that it is hypocritical to oppose hunting and killing with dogs unless one also opposes the killing of animals or fish for the provision of food. In its extreme form, this argument extends to the point where it says that only vegans should oppose hunting, and that for anyone else to do so is hypocritical. The claim can be answered by remarking that killing for food is attitudinally and morally distinct from hunting and killing for sport. Normally, the person who kills for food does the killing as quickly and humanely as possible, so that the creature suffers as little as possible. It does not always happen, of course, which is why the continuing work of organizations such as Compassion in World Farming is so vitally important. But where hunting with dogs is concerned, the enjoyment of the sport actually requires that the process be protracted. As remarked, the lame fox that is killed at once affords the hunt little satisfaction. It is not hypocritical therefore for people who are not vegans to seek an end to the deliberate cruelty of hunting with hounds.

The Changing World of the Family

The opportunities and difficulties of politics and work, the creative opportunity of leisure pursuits, these may be many and various, but they do not take up the whole of our lives. We are also family members, and, for many of us, that membership is fundamental to our lives. But whilst it may be fundamental, it is certainly not unchanging. In the last century, in the years up to about the 1960s, the nuclear family reigned supreme, both in practice and in morality. In the great majority of homes, the two adult partners were married, the husband and father being the wage earner, and the wife and mother the homemaker. Two natural parents living together brought up the children of the marriage. Discipline was firm. Divorce was rare. It was regarded as a disgrace, and, if the previous marriage ceremony had taken place in Church, then it was held to contravene the will of God. Sexual intercourse outside marriage was a sin. Homosexual activities were criminal.

Today the situation is very different. Sexual intercourse between friends but outside marriage is increasingly the norm, particularly among young people who often choose to live together in informal partnerships. The partnership has become a form of relationship akin to marriage, but without the legal commitment of people who are actually married. The idea that sexual activities within such informal partnerships might be sinful is simply not entertained by the participants. The step from friendship to partnership is regarded as sufficient ground in itself for the forming of permanent sexual relationships. Marriage remains popular, nevertheless, but divorce has also become extremely common, and the Churches, if anguished, view it with increasing acceptance. With fewer nuclear families, many children are now brought up in 'single parent families', or in homes in which only one natural parent is present. Some children seem uninfluenced by discipline. Where a man and a woman live together, married or not, both are likely to contribute to the wage earning, and sometimes the woman is the sole earner. Homosexual activities between consenting adults are no longer criminal, and pressure groups seek actively to overcome any kind of discrimination made on grounds of sexual orientation. Putting it all together, there is very little that has remained unchanged.

These changes have been underpinned by a general increase in the liberality of society, or in the permissiveness of society as it is otherwise put. Accompanying these changes, and perhaps in part explaining them, has been a continuing decrease in orthodox religious belief. To repeat a previous argument, an earlier generation largely withdrew from Christian doctrine, but still held on to Christian sexual morality and the family structure. The next generation seems to have taken the logic of the process a step further, rejecting both sexual moral authority and many of the previous conventions of family life.

What is to be made of all these changes? To begin on a positive note, there is much to be welcomed today in the appreciation that individuals should not be criminalized for their private choice of sexual activity, that children born outside wedlock should not be stigmatized, and that couples should not remain trapped in loveless marriages. In similar fashion, the greater opportunity for women to pursue careers is an important step forward from the constraints and prejudices of the past. But of course there is a downside. For some children the lack of a stable nuclear family in which to be nurtured is disastrous. Whilst the break up of families may serve on some occasions to free individuals from wretched relationships, it also frequently brings misery and distress upon both adults and children. In these unstable and difficult circumstances, what is needed is the restoration of the notion of the family as central to both natural and spiritual life.

In this respect, the natural or biological circumstance of humankind is not difficult to understand. Human children need total care in the early months of their lives, and remain in need of nurture at least up to the age of about ten years. They continue to need help for some years thereafter, but from the age of about ten can make some effort to provide for themselves. Given the complete helplessness of the newborn baby, and the long timespan in which essential nurturing continues, it is evident that a minimum of two adults is normally needed to provide for the upbringing of a child. The nuclear family, with one adult working while the other has the direct care of the children, offers a natural way of achieving that basic requirement. Hence the attachment of previous generations to marriage, and to the virtue of confining sexual intercourse to the married state. The value of virginity and the sanctity of marriage were ideas that stemmed directly from a natural state in which children would be born only when an adult structure was already established to provide for them.

It belongs to the nature of a modern affluent and sophisticated society, however, to be able to provide for the material well-being and oversight of children without being dependent upon earlier family structures. But although the outcomes may be materially adequate, it seems that they often fail in other ways. In respect of the family, there is an urgent need for society to look anew at the needs of children, particularly their spiritual needs, and to see what structures can best provide for them. There is also the need to recognize that without spiritual values the benefits of affluence and sophistication in human affairs can all too easily be overstated.

Many Routes

Life on earth is really a myriad of individual lives, each with its own experiences, opportunities and concerns. In corresponding fashion, there is a myriad of spiritual paths, one for each individual human being. But whilst the number is legion, the spiritual themes are common. One way of giving this idea expression is to say that there are many different routes that lead to God. That is to define spirituality in theistic terms, a step that some would refuse to take and others would take but haltingly. But whether or not the spiritual journey is expressed in terms of a journey to God, according to the argument developed in this text the commitments to truth, freedom, caring and reconciliation will form its common constituents. Common too will be the presence of creativity, located in a vast range of individual manifestations. What will be less common, however, is the language. 'Secular spirituality' is not an expression that is likely to be widely used. For people who live almost entirely outside the framework of a religious organization, secular life is just life. 'Secular' as a term is only needed when drawing a distinction from 'religious'. In this country at least, much of what has been termed 'secular spiritual' will simply be rendered 'spiritual'. In itself, this is not a matter of any great significance. Terminology can change, but the important point to make is that spirituality becomes unstructured and weakened if truth, freedom, caring and reconciliation are simply entertained piecemeal in the various aspects of life. Whether or not they are contained under the name 'secular spirituality', the four commitments need to be gathered into a coherent whole if they are to exercise their full influence in human spiritual life.

In a sense, the elements of this chapter form a series of 'for instances' in the field of spirituality. Inevitably, other people will have very different concerns from those that have been ventilated here, or may perhaps share the same concerns but come to different conclusions. But whatever the particular concerns, if the ideas embodied in secular spirituality are to become widely significant, the four principal commitments will need to be accepted in concert and the value of creative endeavour recognized in association.

Notes

1. E. Fitzgerald, *Rubaiyat of Omar Khayyam Done into English*, 1859, Collins Fontana.

2. Thomas Hardy. His novels and poems are frequently expressive of this harsh philosophy. This applies for example in *The Return of the Native* where the gloomy landscape of Egdon Heath provides the grim environment in which men can do little more than endure.

3. Karl Marx, *Critique of the Gotha Programme*, 1875.

4. Cicero, *Pro Milone,* c.110 BC.

5. Geneva Conventions. The four Geneva Conventions of 1949 dealt with matters as follows:

Convention I for the Amelioration of the Condition of the Wounded and Sick in Armed Forces in the Field.

Convention II for the Amelioration of the Condition of Wounded, Sick and Shipwrecked Members of the Armed Forces at Sea.

Convention III Relative to the Treatment of Prisoners of War.

Convention IV Relative to the Protection of Civilian Persons in Time of War.

Preceding the Geneva Conventions, the most comprehensive agreement was the 1907 Hague Convention Respecting the Laws and Customs of War on Land. The question of genocide, whether in war or peace, was considered after World War Two, and, in 1948 the United Nations adopted the Convention on the Prevention and Punishment of the Crime of Genocide. In 1977 two Protocols additional to the Geneva Conventions were established. These were:

Protocol I Relating to the Protection of Victims in International Armed Conflicts.

Protocol II Relating to the Protection of Victims of Non-International Armed Conflicts.

Both the United Kingdom and the United States, in signing the Protocols, stated that they did so on the understanding that rules introduced by the Protocols did not regulate or prohibit the use of nuclear weapons.

For a comprehensive text, see A. Roberts and R. Guelff, *Documents on the Laws of War*, Clarendon Press, 1982.

6. Francis Fukuyama, *The End of History and the Last Man*, Penguin Books, 1992.

7. Hernando de Soto, *The Mystery of Capital*, Why Capitalism triumphs in the West and Fails Everywhere Else, Bantam Press, 2000.

8. John Dryden, *The Character of a Good Parson*, 1700.

9. Genesis, 1: 1.

9
Religion

Religious Foundation

The subject matter of this text is fast approaching completion. The quest for truth, together with the commitments to freedom, caring and reconciliation, form the essence of spiritual life in the secular world. What is evident, however, is that none of these spiritual elements is dependent upon an explicitly religious foundation. The same is true of human creativity, which forms the further definitive component of secular spiritual life. In fact, it is possible for modern spirituality to be free-standing, in the sense that it can be taken up simply as a matter of personal choice. A philosophic or religious stance is not a necessity. But whilst that can be true in some cases, it is hardly a frequent occurrence. Doubts on matters of religious belief may be legion, but the outcome is only rarely a total absence of belief. Beliefs or at least hopes are widely sustained that God is the Creator of the world and that life in this world does not constitute the totality of existence. Such beliefs, however, are often held without any explicit association with formal religious doctrine or organized religious activity.

This series of points encompasses and summarizes the principal elements of modern secular spirituality. All that seems strictly needed, therefore, to complete the text is a final chapter, drawing the various strands together and pointing the way into the future. It cannot quite be left like that, however, and for two reasons. First, the religious history of the land renders it inevitable that spirituality in Britain will have its origins in the traditions of British Christianity. To take due cognizance of this point, it is desirable to see just how closely the ideas of modern secular spirituality will in fact relate to Christian orthodoxy. Secondly, it is evident that spirituality in Britain today functions in a pluralist society, with many different world religions participant. Their related activities and beliefs influence the secular world, and touch upon even the most overtly secular of spiritual lives. For an account of modern secular spirituality to be comprehensive, therefore, it must also take cognizance of the pluralism of the contemporary religious scene.

Augustinian and Irenaean Christianity

The risk of confusion in this chapter is considerable. In the first place, as just noted, it already belongs to the argument to include a religious component, in the form of the hope or belief in God the Creator and in eternal life. That being the case, what exactly does the relation of secular spirituality to Christian orthodoxy mean? What it means is the relationship with the principal body of Christian doctrine, as traditionally formulated, the body of doctrine that certainly includes belief in God and eternity, but which also contains a framework of structured beliefs concerning the drama of divine activity and the person of Jesus. That may sound straightforward enough, but the situation is complicated by the fact that Christian doctrine takes so many different forms. To avoid this text becoming overwhelmed with detail, the argument will focus upon two principal Christian themes or forms of belief, both of which are manifest in a number of Christian denominations, including the Church of England. The practice or convention will be followed of naming these two themes after St Augustine [1] and St Irenaeus [2]. Christians of an evangelical persuasion tend to follow the Augustinian theme, whilst the Irenaean theme attracts those with a more liberal approach. In their formularies, the majority of Churches are basically Augustinian, but some in their practices are broad Churches and happily accommodate those whose personal beliefs point in the Irenaean direction. The Anglican Churches certainly exhibit this generous characteristic. In relation to the distinction drawn by Jonathan Clatworthy between optimistic and pessimistic theologies, Irenaean beliefs are chiefly optimistic, whereas Augustinian are almost always pessimistic.[3] The correspondence is not exact, but it can usually be assumed to apply. This is by no means the only way of distinguishing between different forms of Christian belief, but it does seem to be the one that relates most clearly to the notions of secular spirituality. That being said, both the Augustinian and Irenaean forms have a number of variants, of which only the most dominant will be addressed.

The theme of the Augustinian Christian tradition is embodied in the great drama of salvation. The drama begins with the fall of humanity, an act of disobedience to God that brings suffering and death in its wake. It ends with the separation of the human race into the saved and the damned, segregated for eternity in heaven and hell. Within this tradition, the pivotal moment is the crucifixion of Christ, an event which is interpreted as God wanting to save at least some human beings from the consequences of the fall, and accordingly sending his Son to die on the cross as a sacrifice to atone for their guilt.

A succinct account of this form of Christian belief is given by John Hick in *God and the Universe of Faiths*, where it is offered in direct contrast to the Irenaean account. [4] Although not named as 'Augustinian', Paul Badham describes Victorian Christian beliefs in somewhat similar terms, and demonstrates how they contrast with the themes of Modernist theology. Badham suggests that beliefs of this kind were held to be literally true in Victorian times, but that for most Christians today this is no longer the case. [5] Encouraging as that thought is, the latter part of the assessment may need questioning. What Badham describes does seem to bear quite a close resemblance to much that could be heard in some more evangelically minded Churches of the mid-twentieth century. Moreover, the idea of substitutionary atonement continues to this day to be widely offered in the Church as an account of the significance of the crucifixion. And where that idea is held, other Augustinian beliefs are likely to be present in accompaniment.

There are a number of variations upon the general Augustinian or evangelical theme. Those of particular significance can be identified as follows:

(a) Death was introduced into the world, and *a fortiori* into the circumstances of men, as a consequence of human sin. Either this is taken literally as beginning with the sins of Adam and Eve, or collectively as a consequence of the universality of sin among humankind (in which case the sins of Adam and Eve become illustrative). In either case, death is a punishment for sin - the wages of sin! Disease and the hardships of life assume similar functions when viewed as consequences of the flawed relationship between man and God.

(b) Life after death takes several different forms. In the first, death is simply extinction - the wages of sin - and life after death is resurrection life, life only for those who are saved by Christ. In the second variant, every human being will experience life after death, but the outcome is an act of individual judgement, by God or Christ, leading to an eternity in heaven or hell. In a further subdivision, judgement may be given immediately at death, or may occur at the second coming of Christ. In the latter case, judgement is given both for the 'quick and the dead', meaning both those who are alive at the second coming of Christ and those who had previously died.

(c) The life, death and resurrection of Jesus, provide the means of salvation for man - or for some men. According to the Gospel, 'whosoever believeth in him should not perish but have everlasting life'.[6] Upon that basis, the three fundamental requirements for salvation are first faith in Jesus' saving grace, obtained through his sacrifice as the Lamb of God, secondly repentance and thirdly the forgiveness given to others.

At its Augustinian extreme, it is argued that only those who have been chosen by God, his elect, will be given the grace that is necessary to acquire faith in Jesus. Every other human being is in consequence condemned. As beliefs become progressively more generous, however, so the opportunities extend. At the limit of generosity, salvation through Jesus is seen as a gift from God for every human being, whether or not it is the subject of explicit belief.

The essence of the Augustinian position is judgement. The travails of this life and its conclusion in death are to be regarded either as a punishment deriving from a judgement already made, or as a test leading to a judgement to be made at or beyond death. It is a form of Christianity that receives substantial support from certain biblical passages, and provides the basis for a large element of Christian tradition. Undoubtedly, the tendency today is to move toward the more generous interpretations, but just how far that extends is unclear.

The underlying framework of the Augustinian beliefs became the subject of challenge in Victorian times. In fact, it had often been challenged before, but it was the disputes that began in the Victorian era that led to the religious circumstance of today. Broadly the argument proceeds as follows. Although it is the Christian claim that God is Love, the validity of that claim seems to be circumscribed by the Augustinian insistence that He is also the God of Judgement. Edward Fitzgerald made this objection repeatedly and eloquently in his poetic translation of the *Rubaiyat of Omar Khyyam*, of which a single line will suffice:

'Sue for a Debt we never did contract'. [7]

Why believe in a form of judgement by God that would be quite unacceptable in any human relationship, and about which the human race seemingly has no choice? Can love be given its highest expression by an action intended to set aside such a judgement? The evidence of daily life is that where love is primarily in evidence, judgement only appears if circumstances render it unavoidable. No member of a happily married couple or loving family would even start to make the kind of sweeping condemnatory judgements of which God is supposedly the author. Love accepts the frailties of the loved one, seeks to care for the loved one, and desires the presence of the loved one. Departure into hell is not an option. So why does God reach such a position, and then have to put it right through the life, death and resurrection of Jesus? From Victorian times onward, the force of this kind of moral questioning gradually weakened the previous hold of Augustinian belief.

The second issue stems from the first, and concerns the interpretation of the crucifixion as substitutionary atonement. This has already been examined at length in Chapter 7, and it will not be necessary to repeat the argument that was then made. Suffice it to say that, whilst affirming the utter and fundamental importance of reconciliation in spiritual life, for many people today it is no longer credible to make it depend upon an act of vicarious sacrifice.

The liberal Irenaean tradition differs fundamentally from the Augustinian. To distinguish the concepts, Augustinian Christianity places a heavy emphasis upon events – the divine drama in which Jesus, by his sacrifice, averts the wrath of God from (some of) the human race. The drama is not only demonstrational and inspirational, it is real and effective; salvation is only possible because of it. In contrast, the liberal Irenaean position is established, not chiefly upon events, but upon what are perceived as the eternal truths about the nature of God, in particular his infinite capacity for love and forgiveness. The dominant Irenaean theme is love, not judgement. Indeed, judgement in the direct Augustinian sense hardly rates a mention. The travails of this life and its conclusion in death constitute an opportunity - not a punishment or a trial. Man has not fallen from some previous state of innocence, but is a creature of God in a state (at least a potential state) of spiritual development. Christians (in the Irenaean mould) are those whose spiritual development has been inspired by the life, death and resurrection of Jesus.

Given its liberal nature, it is inevitable that the theme of Irenaean Christianity should have a number of variations. An enthusiastic and detailed account is given by John Hick, who defines its general character by describing human life as a pilgrimage, with bodily death forming the transition from one stage to the next. Whereas, according to the Augustinian perception this world has fallen from a previous paradisal state, in the contrasting Irenaean view it is in a state of development, affording human beings the opportunity to live as moral beings and to begin realizing their spiritual potential. Given the breadth of opportunity embodied in the Irenaean worldview, it becomes possible to accommodate the many different beliefs that liberal Christians have upheld in their varying circumstances.

This approach provides a welcome link between modern secular spirituality and the traditions of Christianity that are inescapably included in the origins of spiritual life in Britain. Within its framework, Hick also opens the door to relations with the other principal faiths that are now to be found in this pluralist country. Yet there are still problems with the Irenaean beliefs - as well as with the Augustinian beliefs - and these need now to be examined.

Since the notions of God's wrath and Jesus' atoning sacrifice have caused such acute difficulty in modern times, the contrasting attraction of the Irenaean position seems self-evident. So what gives reason to pause? One answer is a lack of certainty as to what extent the Irenaean version of Christianity should properly be termed 'Christian' at all. Of course, there is a sense in which words can be used as one chooses - definitions are not fixed but change according to usage. But that is a facility to use with caution. The thought remains that Augustinian Christianity is in large measure Christianity according to Bible and tradition, and that there is too much natural theology – albeit of a strongly liberal character - in what is termed 'Irenaean'. Upon that argument, Augustinian Christianity is authentic Christianity, and the further reaches of what has been identified as 'Irenaean Christianity' should more accurately be described as post-Christian. It needs to be remarked, however, that there is a strong contrary view to this. Some liberal theologians argue that modern biblical scholarship does not support St Augustine's understandings, and that it is the Irenaean tradition that has stronger biblical grounds for its claim to be authentically Christian. This point is not going to be pressed to a conclusion in this text. Instead, whilst associating the arguments relating to modern secular spirituality with the understandings of Irenaean Christianity, the question will be left open as to whether either or both should be termed post-Christian rather than Christian. Whatever the outcome, the more significant point to emerge is that secular spirituality is far removed from all but the most generous interpretations of Augustinian Christianity. In contrast, it is seen to approach much more closely to the Irenaean theme, with its inclusive character and its concept of the nature of spiritual development.

Two further points also seem pertinent to the issue of religious orthodoxy. The first is a reminder of earlier concerns about revelation. One does not have to be cynical about revelation in general, or disposed to follow the Deists in dismissing it entirely from religious belief, in order to express doubt about some of the alleged revelatory messages in the Bible. To mention once again an Old Testament example, the claim that God provides rules for the treatment of slaves constitutes an occasion when it is reasonable to question whether the revelation was real or was simply announced in order to give Divine authority to regulations that society was being asked to accept. That is a single and perhaps extreme example, but it serves nevertheless to illustrate a general point. In the pursuit of truth, both care and caution are needed in the acceptance of recorded revelation. Clearly, such caution accords more readily with the Irenaean tradition than the Augustinian, and its acceptance tends to strengthen the relationship of that tradition with the more secular forms of spirituality.

The second issue concerns reconciliation. While people may grasp its importance pragmatically in the business of daily life, in this country its theological origin is very largely Christian. So the spiritual importance of reconciliation, and its associated contribution to the idea of life after death – both of these arise from a Christian heritage. Yet as previously discussed in Chapter 7, the very doctrines of the Church that relate to reconciliation are those that create some of the worst difficulties for people today. Issues of judgement and hell-fire, sacrificial lambs and beliefs necessary for salvation, all these combine to create uncertainty extending to outright disbelief in a society that questions the morality of vengeance, rejects the notion of sacrificial slaughter, and supports the individual pursuit of objective truth. The role of Biblical revelation in establishing that reconciliation is essential for spiritual well-being needs to be properly acknowledged, yet the manner in which contemporary understanding differs from traditional Christian doctrine must also be given due weight. This creates a certain tension – but it is a tension that needs to be openly admitted, as the account of the relationship between Christian religious spirituality and modern secular spirituality will otherwise be inaccurate and incomplete.

Pluralism

The presence of different faiths is an important feature of the contemporary English community. In respect of spirituality, this modern pluralism can lead to a polarization of attitudes. For those active in their religious organizations, one possible reaction is to put up a strong resistance to the influence of other faiths. This can involve placing a particular emphasis on whatever makes the chosen religion distinctive or unique. In Christian terms, this most easily finds expression in the further reaches of Augustinian belief, where the notion of the 'elect of God' is available to provide comfort and confidence. More widely in the world, and not confined to any particular religion, defensive attitudes can all too easily lead to religious intolerance. If fused with racial intolerance, the resulting mixture can be deadly. Recent examples of this unhappy outcome are not difficult to find.

Still focusing upon persons active in religious activity, the other possibility is almost exactly the opposite. It centres upon inter-faith dialogue, the deliberate seeking out and celebrating of what is common in different faiths. It also includes the endeavour to understand and respect whatever is essentially different. In Christian terms, it is characterized by the inclusive modes of Irenaean thought, a way forward that is given particularly vigorous advocacy by John Hick.

But what influence does pluralism have upon secular spirituality? Once again, there seem to be two answers, one positive and one negative. Dealing with the negative first, the presence of different beliefs may simply add to the opportunities for confusion. At least in days of yore, people knew what it was that they did not believe, or were not sure about! Nowadays, as the scope for disbelief grows ever larger, so the temptation can grow to resist confusion by dismissing all possible religious beliefs. But that is only the negative side. The alternative positive option is to find in the diversity of religions the provision of greater and richer opportunities for individual spiritual development. The greater the variety and depth of religious insight that is available in the land, the greater the choice for the individual in establishing his or her spiritual path.

In the working out of the positive and negative options, the crucial element is the commitment to freedom and human rights. Where that commitment is strong, the social and religious environment will facilitate inter-faith dialogue, and individuals can enjoy the benefit of differing insights. But if the commitment is weak, the outcome can be religious strife, which, at its worst, becomes sufficient to tear whole communities apart. The recent conflict in Bosnia stands as a terrible example.

In terms of the well-being of the community, it would seem therefore that the spiritual commitment to freedom and human rights assumes a quite critical role when a diversity of religions is present. It has been previously argued that the commitment is an essential element for the spiritual journey of individual human beings. What now emerges is the social dimension. The commitment to freedom and human rights constitutes the essential accompaniment of religious pluralism, if societies are to remain cohesive and individual opportunities for spiritual development are to be realized.

The Church

So far in this chapter, it has not been necessary to focus attention directly upon the nature of religious organizations. Where the Christian religion is concerned, however, the Church is of far greater doctrinal significance than any mere organization, and its role in relation to modern spirituality needs some exploration. That being said, neither the issues raised nor the responses to them are intended to be at all comprehensive. They are limited to just two aspects of doctrine that became prominent in the twentieth century and that seem to impinge particularly strongly upon the ideas of secular spirituality.

The first is associated with the concept of the Church as given by Karl Barth [8]. Arguably the most important Protestant evangelical theologian of the twentieth century, Barth derived many of his arguments from Calvin, and they seem to resonate with much that is most potent in the Augustinian tradition. According to Barth, the Church is composed of the body of persons predestined by God for eternal life. Whilst this does not mean that the Church is to be identified directly with the Kingdom of God, it does mean that those persons who constitute the Church during their earthly lives will at the last become the members of the Kingdom of God. It follows that the Church itself is a temporal earthly body leading those who are chosen by God toward their eternal destiny in the Kingdom. Barth also regarded the Church as being the subject of faith, not just of sight. This seems to mean that whilst the Church certainly includes those persons who belong to its assembled congregations it also encompasses some others whom God has chosen but who are not yet visibly its members.

Neither predestination nor Barth's vision of the salvation of the elect relate at all comfortably to the notions of a secular spirituality. In particular, his concept of the function of the Church contrasts with that of secular organizations that advance the cause of freedom and human rights. The latter organizations argue for the conferment of human rights upon every human being – not just upon those who believe in upholding them. (In logic, they must argue like that. Otherwise they would not be pursuing human rights, only the rights of a limited group.) Clearly, if the Church is viewed as a body that only embraces the elect of God, it must exhibit very different characteristics. To make sense of an elect, there also has to be an 'unelect' who by definition do not belong to the Church and cannot even be helped. Barth does offer a greater liberality in the proposition that the Church of faith is accounted for only in part by its visible members. In this context, it is normally assumed that it is only God who identifies those other members, and it is not for human beings to know who they are. From that position, it would only require a single (although very large) step beyond the notion of 'invisible' members to reach the idea of the love of God extending to the whole of humankind. But of course an advance of that kind would also involve the abandonment of the notion of exclusivity arising from belief in the Church as the elect of God. Therein would lie not so much an extension as a departure from the Augustinian theme as expressed by Barth.

The second issue is less acute but subtler. It can be illustrated from the work of the writer C. S. Lewis, who offered a simpler and more generous vision of the Church.[9] The Church is the Body of Christ, and being a member of the Body of Christ means sharing in the Christ-life. The Christ-life is spread within individual members by baptism, belief and Holy Communion. As explained by Lewis, the Christian belief is that those who share in the Christ-life also share in His conquest of death and find a new life beyond it. However, for persons to share the Christ-life means much more than following His teaching or behaving morally. It means that Christ actually operates through them.

This last point occasions the difficulty. Only some people will take up the kind of beliefs necessary for the sharing of the Christ-life. There is also the question of what Christ is believed to be doing when He operates through those who do share His life? Christians have no monopoly of morality or of love. In any case, according to Lewis the sharing of the Christ-life is not just a matter of being morally upright or loving. In practice, identifying and distinguishing the Christ-life in ordinary daily life is not at all easy, and there is a natural tendency to seek it instead in the worshipping activities of the Church. Congregational worship seems to provide more easily recognized occasions for the distinctive nature of the Christ-life to become manifest. The problem is that, however unintentionally, such an approach to the Christ-life has the tendency to downgrade spiritual life in the secular world. Given the thrust of the previous argument, that is not a notion that encourages. What is needed for this argument is a vision of the Church that can uphold, inform and inspire secular spirituality, rather than minimize it.

It may be objected that the ideas put forward by Barth and Lewis are by no means representative, and that choosing them exaggerates the problems of the relationship between Church and society. Furthermore, it can be claimed that liberal Irenaean interpretations of the Christian faith lead to very different visions of the Church. The objections are serious and need a careful response. The justification for choosing the ideas of Barth and Lewis is that their concepts of the Church, whilst clearly not universal, are certainly not uncommon. Where such ways of thinking are present, they lead inescapably to the kind of problems that have been described. To make this point is not to deny either the strength or the importance of liberal modes of thought in the Church; it is simply an attempt to explain the nature of the problem, where it occurs.

Christianity and Secular Spirituality

Putting the previous arguments together, to what extent do the forms of secular spirituality that have been slowly assembled in previous chapters relate to Christian belief and Church practice? Clearly, the answer differs markedly depending upon which of the two principal Christian traditions is being addressed.

Beginning with the Augustinian position, ideas of universal condemnation and substitution atonement sit uncomfortably in the modern world. Likewise, the concepts of the divine drama seem unconvincing. It seems that a great many people in the British population today are swayed by these difficulties. Whatever the explanations offered for the absence of individuals from the pew, the probable underlying reason is that the divine drama, as proclaimed to previous ages, is simply not credible today. There are two parts to this. Firstly, modern concepts of morality and love are such that believing in a God of love does not any longer seem consistent with believing in His supposed wrath and condemnation. Secondly, modern concepts of reconciliation do not seem consistent with vicarious suffering.

With regard to the four commitments of secular spirituality - the commitments to truth, freedom, caring and reconciliation - their relationship with Augustinian Christianity is evidently not at all comfortable. If one particular set of beliefs is necessary for salvation, then the pursuit of objective truth is not the point. Freedom and human rights have little to do with discovering the way to avert the wrath of God. Caring and reconciliation as understood today, are not consistent with notions of condemnatory judgement and substitution atonement.

The situation becomes, of course, quite different when considering the Irenaean or liberal understanding of Christian doctrine. The commitment to truth is a centrepiece of Irenaean thought. Although there is not quite the same emphasis upon freedom and human rights that is found in a chiefly secular spirituality, there is no inconsistency either. The commitment to caring is happily common. What is noticeable, however, in liberal Christian thinking, is the comparative lack of attention afforded to reconciliation. In setting aside the necessary causal link between salvation and crucifixion that characterizes Augustinian belief, Irenaean thought tends instead to focus directly upon caring and compassion, and has a tendency to play down the significance of repentance and forgiveness. If liberal Christian thinking is to illuminate secular spirituality, this is a feature that needs to change. Important as it is to reject substitution atonement, or any other causal linking of salvation to the cross, the Christian recognition of the absolute significance of reconciliation does need to be upheld. No doubt there are different ways in which this could be attempted. To align with the thrust of the argument in this text, one approach would be to view the sacrifice of Jesus strictly within its first century Jewish context. For a society that was brought up (spiritually speaking) on the idea of sacrifice as a means of atonement, the acceptance by Jesus of his own crucifixion led his disciples to place reconciliation at the very forefront of their spiritual lives. Beginning with that kind of perception, it should be possible for the liberal Christian thinker today not so much to demythologize the biblical account as to work within it in order to draw out the essential message of reconciliation.

Returning finally to the question of the Church or Churches, the commitments and beliefs of secular spirituality have been shown to be broadly consistent with those of liberal Irenaean Christianity. They do not, however, relate at all satisfactorily to Augustinian beliefs, and this creates difficulty where Church membership is concerned. Although a number of denominational Churches would claim to hold doctrinal positions broad enough to admit adherents of both the Augustinian and Irenaean traditions, there is a continuing tendency for the language of Augustinian Christianity to be dominant in worship. There are many people for whom this form of language will prove a convincing deterrent to a seat in the pew, and, in consequence, the theistic beliefs associated with modern spirituality will often continue to be held in separation from any organized religious body.

Notes

1. St Augustine of Hippo, Christian theologian and philosopher, AD 54-430.
2. St Irenaeas, early father of the Church, c. AD140-200.
3. Jonathan Clatworthy, *Good God*, Jon Carpenter Publishing, 1997.
4. John Hick, *God and the Universe of Faiths*, Oneworld Publications, 1993.
5. Paul Badham, *The Contemporary Challenge of Modernist Theology*, University of Wales Press, 1998.
6. John, 3: 16.
7. E Fitzgerald, *Rubaiyat of Omar Khyyam Done into English*, 1859, Collins Fontana.
8. Karl Barth, *The Faith of the Church*, 1943, Translated by Gabriel Vahanian, Collins Fontana, 1967.
(9) C. S. Lewis, *Mere Christianity*, Collins Fontana, 1960.

10

Destiny

Spirit

What conclusions can be drawn from these various wonderings? How does it all assemble, if it assembles at all? In exploring the spiritual nature of humankind, attention has focused upon modern secular spirituality, with truth, freedom, caring and reconciliation identified as its principal commitments. Beginning with truth, an early point to grasp is the extent of uncertainty in life, an uncertainty that pervades both philosophy and religious belief, and adds acutely to the difficulties of choosing a spiritual path. Truth is correspondence with the facts, and in a world of great and abiding mystery the facts are often hidden from us. The resulting uncertainties can be painful. Attending the funeral some years ago of a much loved cousin who had died quite suddenly and unexpectedly, I was asked after the ceremony to join members of the family at the house of a close relative. As we gathered in the front room, a young man who had been present at the ceremony sighed and remarked: 'Well, if there is nothing more, at least it was quick.' There was a general murmur of assent round the room. The harsh truth is that there is no certainty of life beyond the one that we know on this earth. That is not to question the sincerity of the prayers that had been uttered at the cremation ceremony, but it is to recognize that many of the people who had gathered there entertained the idea of eternal life more in hope than in confidence.

Death is not the only great mystery, although it may be the most melancholy. Why am I the one person that I am among the billions of people that inhabit the earth? Why I am here on planet earth at all, and was planet earth itself created or did it just happen? Why is it that time flows in only one direction, and what will the future hold? In general, any commitment that I make to follow truth must begin by acknowledging just how few questions I can actually answer.

But in offering these austere remarks, it is knowledge that is under scrutiny, not belief or hope. The more enthusiastically that philosophers, schooled in epistemology and logic, chip away at the tree of knowledge, the more important it is to recognize the role of belief in human lives. This is important. A little learning at the feet of some modern thinkers, and it is all too easy to slip from a healthy scepticism into a mere cynicism. The point to emphasize, arising from the earlier arguments, is that human beings not only form beliefs upon all manner of subjects, but that it is proper and in many cases virtually essential that they should. But with belief goes doubt! With knowledge in short supply, doubts and beliefs have to coexist, both in everyday affairs and in the great issues of spirituality and religion.

In earlier chapters, two principal religious beliefs were explored that coexisted with doubts. The first was the belief that God is the divine Creator of all beings and all things, and the second that human life is eternal, that there is life beyond death. Upon the second assumption, the spirit is the self or person, as he or she becomes after death. The idea of life after death is present in many religions and cultures, but it takes a quite distinct form in this text due to the acceptance of the proposition that the nature of reality is dual.

This is a fundamental point and grows out of the recognition that reality is inexplicable in purely physical terms. To summarize what was said in Chapter 1, if laws that are deterministic or probabilistic govern the physical world, as modern science assumes that they do, then the exercise of free will cannot in itself be an aspect of the physical world. There are two possibilities. Either certain physical entities possess a second set of properties, mental properties, quite unlike those known to physical science, or, alternatively, subjective mental existence occupies a dimension or dimensions quite distinct from those of the physical world. The first possibility, which is a kind of halfway house in the understanding of reality, constitutes an entity monism with an associated property dualism. The second is full entity dualism. It is not possible to say which of the two is correct, only that one of them needs to be, contrary to much that is proffered today as conventional wisdom. In this text, the second option of entity dualism has been preferred, as it is more straightforward and has fewer imponderables. Normally assumed to be the correct choice, it has been liberally applied to the constructive parts of the argument. In so doing, the assumption has also been made that the physical and the mental realms, the body and mind, interact. This interaction takes place at least in the brain, and possibly elsewhere in the body. It enables decisions to be implemented, and allows individual persons to be creative (or destructive) in the physical world. What is important in the context of spiritual life is the recognition that dualism provides a straightforward rationale for life beyond physical death. The life of the spirit after physical death is life in the dimension or dimensions of the mind. There is of course no proof that such a life continues – perhaps the mind dissolves in its own dimension concurrently with the breakdown of the body. But it is entirely rational to think otherwise, and thus to embrace the possibility of spiritual life beyond physical death.

With that possibility as a working assumption, it is pertinent to consider how the mind could function when it floats free of the body. Whilst nothing is certain, some clues can be found by looking at the nature of the self as explored in Chapter 2. At that point it was argued that a person is an holistic being, unable to be explained, systems fashion, as an assembly of parts. A little shamefacedly, a table of the self was then presented, a table bearing a considerable resemblance to a systems presentation. Care was taken, however, to remark that the entries in that table should only be regarded, 'so-to-speak', as illustrating certain aspects of the human character. For convenience of argument, the table in question is repeated below.

ACQUISITION	COGNITION	VOLITION
Perception	Intellect |	Will
	| Reason	
Appetite |	Talent |	Action
| Desire		
Instinct |	Conscience |	
	| *Thymos*	
Emotion	'Heart' |	

Clearly the perceptions of this world, the perceptions that depend for their existence upon the senses of the body (top left in the table), will be lost with death. The capacity for action, physical action by the body in the world (at the further end of the table), will likewise be lost. In contrast, *thymos* and the decision-making will belong wholly within the spirit, and are therefore the obvious candidates for survival. This is asserted on the basis of previous arguments, extending from Chapter 2 to Chapter 9, about the nature of spiritual life. That leaves appetite, instinct, reason and emotion. The appetites belong to the body and depart at death, but, according to the definitions in Chapter 2, although instinct is included with appetite in desire, its precise location is less clear. To avoid complications, it is argued that, insofar as instincts are physical in nature, they depart with the appetite, but where they belong to the mind they are participant in the spirit. With regard to reason and emotion, they too seem to have both physical and mental elements, so their mental elements are likewise included in the spirit. In this text, reason includes creative talent. That being the case, it is the reason and *thymos* that need most emphasis, engaging in the kinds of activity that will constitute the greatest influence on the decisions of the will in the next world.

This notion of the spirit not only accords with the idea of life after death, but is consistent with the Christian belief in resurrection, although clearly not dependent upon it. There is no certainty in the argument, but the dualist position does give to the idea of the on-going spirit a rationality that is absent from wholly physical accounts of life. In Britain, over two thirds of the population describe themselves as Christian. Many will have set aside the formalities of the faith, but in most cases they will still entertain at least a hope in life after death. It is a hope that will often have struggled against the popular conception that life is grounded in a wholly physical reality. That difficulty at least can be set aside on the basis of dualism.

Destiny Here?

There are two quite distinct issues relating to human destiny. The first concerns the future of individuals and of the human race upon this earth. (Given a future of space travel, this could extend to the wider universe.) The second concerns the destiny of individual human beings and of human society beyond this earthly life, in a life belonging to eternity.

In earthbound terms, there is a single common destiny for every individual. We all die! On the whole, it is a destiny about which we prefer not to think, but in the long run it is inescapable. But what is the future of the human race as a whole, as distinct from any one individual? In practice, it is difficult to look any great distance ahead. According to some physicists and cosmologists, the physical universe will eventually run down and cease to be active. Others incline to the view that it will continue indefinitely, first expanding and then contracting, with no recognizable ultimate conclusion. As either possibility would apparently take millions upon millions of years to work out, it is not an issue that requires our most urgent attention! Much more significant is the question of what is going to happen to the human race in the next hundred years or so, the time-span of the next few generations. Within this briefer span, and with the focus chiefly upon spiritual life, it is perhaps reasonable to concentrate attention upon emerging opportunity and risk rather than the prospect of ultimate destiny.

Looking at the recent past, the most important spiritual changes in the western world have comprised a growing concern for truth and freedom, the latter extending to democracy and human rights, and a diminishing acceptance of religious doctrine and practice. Tragically, much of the concern for human rights grew out of the discovery of the utterly appalling events that had stemmed from their absence. Whilst the twentieth century was the century of the Universal Declaration of Human Rights, it was also the century of the Jewish Holocaust.

The political and social thrust, emanating from western countries today, is chiefly in favour of freedom, democracy and human rights, although governmental actions in response to the events of 11 September 2001 have not always supported that endeavour. It would be a comfort to think that western religious influence would be similarly directed toward human rights, and where liberalism is dominant, that has undoubtedly been the case. But, sadly, the influence of liberalism in the Churches has remained somewhat limited. The numerical decline in religious observance has led some of those remaining in active Church membership to seek a defensive refuge in biblical fundamentalism.

This way of thinking was expressed in perhaps its starkest terms by Lord Macaulay, in his History of England. He wrote: 'But the Old Testament contained the history of a race selected by God to be witnesses of his unity and ministers of his vengeance, and specially commanded by him to do many things which, if done without his special command, would have been atrocious crimes.'[1] Of course, those words were written in the nineteenth century and many Christians today would reject them out of hand. Unfortunately, from fairly recent experience of evangelical worship, it seems that others would not, or at least would remain quiescent in a pew whilst the exploits of invading Israelites were enthusiastically recounted.

It seems therefore that the challenge to traditional religious doctrines arising from the movement to uphold human rights needs a substantial response at institutional level. In particular, there are a number of beliefs relating to the Old Testament that need redefining, or at least modifying in their interpretation. As before, these remarks apply chiefly to Britain and the Church of England. In parts of the world where religious fundamentalism holds political sway, however, the struggle for human rights is in an altogether more desperate state. For human society at large, spiritual endeavours on this earth still have a great deal to achieve in the field of human rights.

Any person who assumes that there is a life hereafter will see this world as the cradle of human souls. Wherever our spiritual paths may take us in distant realms, it is from this earth and this life that we start. This earth is and will remain forever our point of departure. Given that assumption, a vital function of spiritual endeavour on earth must be that of creating a suitable environment for spiritual nurture. Questions concerning the destiny of the human race on earth transform into questions concerning the destiny of the cradle of human souls. The total number of human beings in the whole of the human race throughout all its history is not presumably destined to be infinite. In that sense, ultimate destiny, when the last human being has departed, will coincide with the time when this earth ceases to function as a place of human spiritual nurture. What happens then is too far beyond anticipation to be seriously explored. But, in any case, it is of intellectual curiosity only. For as long as the cradle is needed as a cradle, it must be the task of humanity to sustain it. Expressed outside the metaphor but still within its vision, one aim for human society is that of providing the best possible opportunities for spiritual nurture and spiritual life. In the broad context of this argument, it is the aim that defines the principal social role of secular spirituality within the confines of this life and world.

Destiny Hereafter?

Persons upholding Christian beliefs look for the resurrection of the dead. Many others in this land, persons who have stepped aside from the formal doctrines of the Church, still entertain hopes of another life beyond the grave. But the opposite view is also advanced. For example, the poet Edward Fitzgerald warns us that:

'The stars are setting, and the Caravan
Draws to the Dawn of Nothing'[2]

Wherein lies the truth? If we use our time to wonder about the nature of life, are our wonderings at the dawn of nothing or the dawn of eternity? The difference could hardly be more striking. The judgement, belief or doubt, is for each individual to make. It is certainly not the function of this text to offer a definitive answer, but there are pointers that seem relevant.

According to cosmologists, this earth has existed for millions upon millions of years. In comparison, as individual human beings, we are here for only the briefest of spans. We have but a single tiny perspective upon the vastness of it all, yet it belongs to our nature to wonder what it is all about. That our wonderings should leave great areas of doubt and unknowing is hardly surprising. But doubts, however deep and fundamental, are not the same as disbeliefs. Expressions of atheism and pronouncements that this life is the only life are no less dogmatic in their way than the most rigid codifications of religious belief.

Expanding upon these thoughts, destiny normally means whatever is going to happen, whether we like it or not. Does eternity imply a common destiny for all individual human beings, or are there choices? In the view of Fitzgerald, individual human destiny is simply oblivion at death. In that case, it is not only better to travel hopefully than to arrive, it is better to go on travelling as long as possible before arriving – unless life has simply become a misery! But suppose that there is life after death? What form or forms can it be expected to take? Traditional Christian images tend to be more concerned with being than doing. Souls will be 'at rest', 'in peace', 'in heaven', and 'with God'. Christian thinkers were wont to leave it there, probably because of difficulties in identifying anything that they were sure still needed to be done! In contrast, doing is essential in this life, and the term 'essential' is not used casually. If we do not plant crops or otherwise provide for our food, then most of us will very quickly cease to live – on this earth that is! We must take action in order to eat and drink, and, except in the warmest climes, to provide ourselves with clothing and shelter. It is only when we have sustained life itself that we can also act to make life enjoyable, or proceed in search of higher goals.

Looking at biblical images of life on earth, according to the Book of Genesis: 'In the sweat of thy brow shalt thou eat bread, till thou return unto the ground'.[3] Both work and death are understood to be punishments for sin. Life after death is granted with God's forgiveness –

in some respects it is an expression of that forgiveness – so it is hardly surprising that early Christian thinkers should have omitted work from heaven. The end result is that heaven is thought of principally as a place of being rather than doing.

In terms of the argument that has been slowly developing in these chapters, this creates serious problems. The principal commitments of secular spirituality, the commitments to truth, freedom, caring and reconciliation, are all associated with action. A true sentence corresponds with the facts, but if no one ever utters a sentence truth is disengaged. Freedom and human rights are significant only in a life in which things actually happen. Love, compassion, kindness and caring, are all attitudinal, definitive of the spirit in which things are done, but things clearly need to be done if the attitudes are to be given expression! Reconciliation is an activity in itself.

Furthermore, in this world the commitments tend to be assessed by the actions that they prompt. If Tom proclaims to Harry that he cares about Dick, but never actually lifts a finger to help Dick, then Harry may reasonably be sceptical of Tom's claim. If in a broad sense secular spirituality, entailing the commitments to truth, freedom, caring and reconciliation, is to proceed into the next life, then it seems that the next life would need to be one of activity, not simply a state of beatific being. In addition, spirituality is not exhausted by the four listed commitments. Unless the previous arguments are very wide of the mark, tribalism, competition and the need for esteem will also need to be taken up and subsumed into the next life, and they too involve activities. So does creativity, which is essentially active, whether applied in the physical or the mental realm.

If life after death is assumed, then spiritual life bifurcates. The life of the ever changing population of the human race continues on this earth, and the life of the individual spirit continues after death, pursued in whatever form of society may obtain. Beginning with this life, it was argued in Chapter 4 that creation needed to be interesting and fulfilling for its Creator, and freedom and human rights were identified as being essential for that purpose. But more needs to be remarked about the circumstance and time-span. Not everything can be achieved in the brief moment of human life on this earth. It follows that a consideration of the doctrine of eternity is inevitable. In particular, if freedom and other human rights apply only amid the shocks and chances of this present world, then however earnestly they are espoused they will still fall short of the human rights that have formed a vital element of the metaphysical argument. If the metaphysic is to be more than merely fanciful, if the purposes of the Creator are to be regarded as seriously embracing his relationship with humankind, then men and women will need rights and freedoms that transcend this physical universe in order to provide the opportunity for spiritual relationships to develop to the full. The Creator needs therefore to be seen as the ultimate guarantor of the laws that underpin such freedoms. This notion can be expressed through a modern concept of heaven, a concept that posits eternity as the context in which caring relationships can be brought actively to fruition. With such an understanding, the freedom of eternity becomes the freedom to act.

In the development of these points, it is worth adding that the more extreme images of heaven and hell, inhabited by human beings who become wholly good after forgiveness by God or who otherwise remain wholly evil, do not seem to align with the more complex realities of human nature and behaviour. The great majority of human beings are neither thoroughly good nor thoroughly bad. One can argue that the trauma of death and a very different environment will occasion human beings to behave very differently in the next life from the way that they do on this earth. But if it is the spirit that travels into the next world, the spirit that is identifiably the person in the mental realm, then both spiritual strengths and weaknesses will be manifest. Once again, the next world must be expected therefore to be an active world, presenting its own spiritual challenges for individuals to grow in strength and to overcome weakness.

Returning to an earlier theme, it is possible for all the four principal commitments of modern spiritual life, truth, freedom, caring and reconciliation, the four upon which attention has been focused, to be found in a secular setting. Indeed, they can become the goals of a spiritual journey in a wholly this-worldly environment, equally meaningful to humanist, atheist and sceptic. But they can also be placed in a comprehensive setting, related to the belief in God the Creator and aligned with the opportunities of life not only in this world but in the next. Within such a metaphysical framework, the argument can also be offered in converse form. The four principal commitments of modern spirituality, summarized as truth, freedom, caring and reconciliation, can be seen as forming just those aspects of human life that are destined by God to be paramount in the hereafter, following their emergence and nurture in the present. As such, they stand in stark contrast to the material and economic aspects of this present life that 'you cannot take with you'.

Pursuing the nature of a future life still further, and looking first at the commitment to truth, there is a tendency to assume that this is only a temporal problem, as in the next world all truths will swiftly be revealed. Perhaps this will be so, but then again perhaps it will not! What needs to be asserted is that the pursuit of truth, understood as essential for spiritual life in this world, will continue to occupy a vital position in whatever spiritual realm it is being exercised, until the process of discovery is complete. For the remaining commitments, their juxtaposing is not without significance. Freedom is the essential prerequisite of love, whether in this world or in any other. Love that is coerced is simply not love! So freedom, protected by human rights, is a necessary condition for any life in which caring and compassion are to grow and triumph. The point needs to be made with precision. Coercion, applied to uphold human rights and ensure that freedom is not denied, may be unavoidable. Coercion to impose love is unthinkable. And it needs to be added that where there is freedom there is by definition scope for dissent. Love cannot be guaranteed. Neither can it be predicted what desires or imperatives may be found in some other realm in place of those with a biological origin, nor can it be known how their satisfaction may be related to the exercise of freedom. But the fourth commitment of modern secular spirituality, the commitment that stems most evidently from its Christian heritage, is reconciliation. Unless or until individuals radically change, the possibility will remain of freedom being exercised in ways that lack caring and compassion. But if what has been argued is true, it also belongs to the fundamental nature of spirituality for the path of reconciliation to remain open.

The commitments of secular spirituality do not constitute the entirety of spiritual life. In meeting the spiritual challenges of the hereafter, human spirits will be free (must be free) to exercise the will in decision-making, and creativity may be expected to become an increasingly important aspect, surpassing its function on earth. As we saw at the beginning of this argument, decision-making can be creative (or destructive) in the physical world, transcending the scientific law. Being free of the constraints of law, the possibilities of creative endeavour in a future spiritual life may extend beyond the furthest reaches of present imagination. Even within our earthly boundaries, the scope of creativity is immense – from sculptures to symphonies, from epic poems to country gardens. In the context of eternity, we are still moving towards the dawn and the range of spiritual opportunity is hardly yet in view.

Yet however distant the view, it still belongs to our nature to wonder. How does it all end? What is the ultimate purpose and what is human destiny? Perhaps it does not end. Making use of the traditional language of Christianity, it may be that 'glory' is the right word to describe what is striven for, but perhaps the pursuit of glory constitutes an end, even a destiny, in a purposive rather than a temporal sense. Speculating on this theme, it may be that in a realm beyond or outside time the relationship between being and doing changes, so that the two become moulded into a spiritual unity. In that sense, the journey of the spirit may not be a journey to a specific destination beyond which one does not travel, but a journey in which the value is ultimately discovered in the journeying itself. Were that the case, the end or purpose of spiritual life would become united with the creative activity of that life, and the activity would become one with the nature and state of the active spiritual being.

Is this still wondering or is it tending toward fantasizing? Is it fantasizing already? It is difficult to be sure. Doubts have been present throughout this argument. Given their persistent influence, is it even sensible to extend these explorations toward ultimate purpose and destiny? After so many cautionary comments, is there any value in constructing an extensive edifice of thought if a lack of certainty undermines its very foundations? But the semi-rhetorical question addresses only one aspect of the argument. It has also been shown that the role of doubt is not merely negative. Interpreted optimistically, it has the positive function of encouraging respect for and interest in other beliefs (and doubts). As such, the development of any one line of thought, however far-reaching, need not be inhibited. What doubt imposes is the humble recognition that the outcome of any particular argument has no guarantee of being right.

Concluding then on a note of hopeful conjecture rather than confident assertion, the argument focuses for one last time upon the idea of ultimate destiny. Suppose that in some future life the commitments to truth, freedom, caring and reconciliation have been completed and fulfilled. Suppose moreover that the influences of tribalism, competition and esteem have been sublimated and integrated within them. What happens then? Jonathan Clatworthy argues that purposes and values are diverse and progressive.[4] His arguments chime with human aspiration. Perhaps the four commitments and three influences, given their different expression among individual souls, are sufficient in themselves to allow an indefinite diversity and progression. Perhaps with the inclusion of creativity some further and higher goal emerges in which relations between God and humankind continue to grow – a goal which we can best describe as glory. For the present, it does not seem appropriate to attempt a greater precision. What we have is the opportunity to travel in hope upon this earth and to project upon a distant future the possibilities we have glimpsed. In the words of the poet Henry Vaughan:

'So some strange thoughts transcend our wonted themes
And into glory peep.'[5]

That is as far as these wonderings go, reaching toward possibilities that transcend human hopes but are beyond immediate understanding.

Notes

1. Lord Macaulay, *History of England*, 1849–1861, Heron Books, 1967, vol. 1, p. 63.
2. Edward Fitzgerald, *Rubaiyat of Omar Khyyam Done into English* [1859], Collins Fontana.
3. Genesis 3:19.
4. Jonathan Clatworthy, *Good God*, Jon Carpenter Publishing, 1997, ch. 10.
5. Henry Vaughan, *Silex Scintillans*, 1650–5.